Rich Wounds

*An Eternal Perspective
on Suffering*

Sharon Buss

Engeltal Press
P.O. Box 447
Jasper, AR 72641

Table of Contents

Introduction

"Rich wounds yet visible above, in beauty glorified." These words from the song, "Crown Him with Many Crowns," by Matthew Bridges, have been made so real to me through the years. More and more I have been given to understand that the sufferings of our Saviour have all been for our sake, to deliver us from all our pain, shame, bitterness and wounds.

Early in my walk with the Lord, my heart was captured by Philippians 3:10: "That I may know Him, and the power of His resurrection, and the fellowship of His sufferings, being made conformable unto His death." So, I have sought to truly know Him in all of the aspects of His life and death, to conform to Him and take on His shape and likeness.

Adam was made in the image of God, perfect in all aspects. His fellowship with His Father was perfect and without flaw or outside influence. When disobedience marred that relationship, deception and evil became a part of the picture that mankind has beheld on a daily basis. As the result of eating of the tree of the knowledge of good and evil, man became as *elohim*. The Hebrew word *elohim* not only means God or god, it also means judge, and eating that fruit put man in a position to judge, discern, and choose between good and evil. Ever since then, we are constantly having to judge whether something is good or evil and to decide which one to choose in any given moment. We were not designed for such stress! How often we have been deceived and have suffered great loss and wounding as a result of a wrong choice! Don't you just hate it when you realize that you've been duped?

Many of our woundings come at least in part from our own missing of the mark in some way. Pride (the same sin that caused Lucifer to fall) brings a separation from God,[1] putting the proud in great danger. Rebellion is as witchcraft[2] and has a death sentence on it.[3] Unforgiveness is a ticket to Hell.[4] When we are out of line with the Lord, we are a target for wounding.

Some woundings come from those we love, for in opening our hearts to love a person, we give them access to at least a part of our soul. We begin to let down our defenses. Once wounded, however, we tend to draw back and limit access to our hearts, and we begin to shut down our willingness to give love. That is precisely why the accuser of the brethren (the devil, the forever loser) is so intent upon causing wounds. After all, his job description is to kill, steal and destroy (John 10:10). He wants to destroy our likeness to our Heavenly Father by causing all manner of pain. His earnest intent is to take as many of us to Hell with him as he can.

But some of the most devastating wounds come in our childhood through no fault of our own. In His kindness toward us, God even enables us to block out the memories of the traumas and woundings that as children we don't

---

1   "Though the Lord be high, yet has He respect unto the lowly: but the proud He knows afar off." (Psalm 138:6)

2   "For rebellion is as the sin of witchcraft, and stubbornness is as iniquity and idolatry." (1 Samuel 15:23)

3   "Whosoever he be that does rebel against your commandment, and will not hearken unto your words in all that you command him, he shall be put to death..." (Joshua 1:18)

4   "But if you forgive not men their trespasses, neither will your Father forgive your trespasses." (Matthew 6:15)

understand. It's a coping mechanism to shield us from pain.

One of a Kind

God made each of us to be unique. We each have a unique DNA; we were cast into a unique environment, overlaid with a unique set of experiences. Even siblings with the same parents, growing up together in the same circumstances and events will be affected differently and will process their memories uniquely.

When I get together with my siblings, I find it interesting to hear the different details we each remember and don't remember about the same events we experienced together as children. For this reason, I will not give all of the circumstances of the wounds I have received in my life, so that you, dear reader, may apply my experience to your own woundings. The purpose of this writing is not to share my wounds, but to share the healings I have received through the revelation of God's greater purposes being played out through them.

Welcome the Holy Spirit right now to open your soul to receive the healing virtue that was poured out from God through His Isaiah 53 "Suffering Servant," Nazareth's Yeshua ben Yosef, the Son of David, the Root from dry ground.

Some people become bitter toward God from the woundings they received as though He hadn't been there to protect them. He certainly was there, and He ached with you in your pain. He saw to it that your life was spared so that you could be healed and restored. But He gave mankind free will, and hurt people tend to hurt other people. Their woundedness causes them to wound others. The father of lies/accuser whips them up into emotions that overtake their reasoning, and they can become violent without even realizing it.

A few of these chapters contain pertinent readings from my journals. Receiving a personal message from the Lord brings understanding and healing. I trust that His words that ministered to me will also minister to you.

God remains the Creator and Supreme Sovereign of all creation, and in His great love, goodness, and mercy He has prepared a way to turn the most horrific experiences of our lives into good—greater good than we would have had if the experience hadn't happened in the first place.

Allow the wounds of your life to be opened up by your loving Heavenly Father to be healed, beautified, and even glorified.

As you let the Lord bring healing to your woundings, learn to let His armor defend you from future injuries. Learn how to heal quickly by using the Word of God. You will find some keys for this in these pages.

This book has been incubating in my spirit for decades. I have been studying the Word and learning on this subject, gleaning stories that fit, and receiving revelation from the Lord. Hence this volume is better for having waited. Like good wine or cheese, the aging process has produced a maturity in this message that I hope will bring a blessing to you and to the Body of Christ. May it abound to His great glory for ever and ever, Amen!

Sharon Buss

Chapter 1

The Vision

The trip was delightful. Visiting a nation on a far-away continent for the first time has always been exciting to me. This particular journey held an additional layer beyond most of my travel experiences. This time I was going to see an old friend whom I had not seen nor scarcely heard from in many years. My feeling was a mix of delighted anticipation and fear. Our parting years earlier had been under difficult and painful circumstances. We had been very close, but a rift had put time and distance between us.

We were to meet at a conference that would have wonderful spiritual depth of experience. I had no idea at the time how deeply I would be touched and how significant it would be. I waited at the door for my old friend and barely recognized her. Her appearance had changed somewhat and she now wore glasses, but when she smiled, I knew it was her. We met one another with warm, but casual greetings. The meeting was starting, so we proceeded to find seats and settle in our places.

As the praise and worship started, I began to weep with deep, heaving sobs. It was as though God's can opener had begun to cut into the sealed compartment of the grief to which I had never allowed expression. My immediate sarcastic thought was, "Oh, this is going to be really fun—blubbering like this through the whole conference!"

Then the vision began. I saw in the spirit as though my whole midsection had been gouged out. The wound was roughly the size of a large reference Bible, only the sides were sloping. At the depth of the cutout, I could see that there was a layer of muscle that was intact and unharmed, but the edges of the wound were raw and bloody as though fresh.

Then I saw gold dust begin to fall into the open wound and at that very moment the worship leader said, "I see gold dust falling." It began to cover the raw areas and merged together to form a solid gold base, as though it had been formed from molten gold. It looked like the setting for a gemstone.

Then a large, red gemstone appeared above me. It had an emerald-shaped cut, and it was the same size and shape as the gold setting in the wound. When the gemstone settled into place, my weeping stopped, and so did the grief. The vision ended and I was in peace, and proceeded to enjoy the conference.

As the days went on, I came to the end of my resources to be able to give in the offerings. Then I remembered the red jewel I had received in the vision, and decided to do a "prophetic act" by faith to give it to the Lord. I walked to the front, motioning with my hands as to remove it, then placed it on the altar with the offerings that were being given. As I laid it down by faith, I saw in my spirit a diamond of the same size and shape settled into my midsection to take the place of the red one I had removed.

Some nine months later I was in another meeting and the Holy Spirit was challenging us all to make a deeper commitment to the Lord and really give our all. I thought,

"Lord, I've already given You my life. I'm serving You full time. I don't have any financial resources to give You in this moment. What more can I give?"

Immediately I remembered the diamond that had filled up the space where the deep wound had been. I was joyful that I had something of value to offer. By faith I removed the diamond and lifted it up to the Lord. Then I realized that the place where the wound had been was healed, whole, and fully restored. I no longer needed a gemstone as a "placeholder."

At some point in my ponderings of this series of visions I was reminded of the third verse of the old hymn, "Crown Him with Many Crowns" that says, "Rich wounds yet visible above, in beauty glorified." We are told by those who have visited Heaven that the wounds that Jesus bore for us are still visible, but they are beautiful.

Hopelessness on Steroids

On the day that Jesus was crucified, no human being living would have been able to foresee the glory that would come from the horrific, devastating cruelty that He suffered. All those who were convinced that He was the Messiah were certain that God's great plan to deliver them from Rome was somehow being aborted by a vicious enemy. Their hopes had been ravaged and destroyed.

Even the devil himself couldn't foresee it because our wise and loving Heavenly Father had hidden it. This is made clear in 1 Corinthians 2:7-8, "But we speak the wisdom of God in a mystery, even the hidden wisdom, which God ordained before the world unto our glory: Which none of the princes of this world knew: for had they known it, they would not have crucified the Lord of glory."

I can just imagine how satan and all his minions were rejoicing that they had successfully killed their Divine

11

Adversary! Now they could take the earth completely and drag all of mankind with them to Hell. "Aha! Victory at last!" they exclaimed, as they danced with glee. But what a surprise they had when the Lord of Glory stood up among them and exercised His Sovereign authority, demanding that they turn over the keys to Hell and death (Revelation 1:18). He led captivity captive and gave gifts to mankind in the process (Ephesians 4:8-10).

While receiving all the demonic cruelty they could dish out, Jesus was paying the price of human disobedience all the way back to Adam and forward to future generations. "And you, being dead in your sins and the uncircumcision of your flesh, has He quickened together with Him, having forgiven you all trespasses; Blotting out the handwriting of ordinances that was against us, which was contrary to us, and took it out of the way, nailing it to His cross; And having spoiled principalities and powers, He made a show of them openly, triumphing over them in it" (Colossians 2:13-15).

In the same way that a victorious general would parade his conquered and captive foes through the streets to demonstrate his victory and their shame, Jesus exposed the devil in an open show in the spiritual realm, leaving them devastated and trembling at the thought of the judgment yet to come.

"For this purpose the Son of God was manifested, that He might destroy the works of the devil" (1 John 3:8b).

Meanwhile, Back at the Upper Room...

For three days the disciples were in unimaginable grief and mourning. Their Master had been killed and they presumed that they would be next. While they wept and moaned over their loss, they feared every odd sound, wondering if the Sanhedrin would issue orders for them to be rounded up and imprisoned or killed as well. They sat mourning through the Holy Day of the Passover, the next day being the Holy Day of the Feast of Unleavened Bread, then the Sabbath. In their sorrow they forgot that Jesus said He would be in the tomb for three days and three nights. It was three days of agony for the personal loss of their Friend, loss of their hopes and dreams—everything they believed in!

But early in the morning on the first day of the week, the women who loved Him went to the tomb to add some spices to His corpse to make the smell more tolerable while they wept over their loss in the presence of His body. They had loved Him, and finally after the holy days were passed, they could visit His mortal remains.

While the women were discovering the empty tomb and receiving the angels' message that "He is not here, for He is risen," in the nearby barley fields, men were gathering a sheaf of the first ripened stalks of grain to take to the temple for the priests to wave before God. It was the Feast of Firstfruits—in Hebrew, *bikkurim* which comes from the word that means first born. Colossians 1:18 refers to Him as "the firstborn from the dead." And 1 Corinthians 15:20-21 gives more understanding of God's purposes: "But now is Christ [Messiah] risen from the dead, and become the firstfruits of them that slept. For since by man came death, by man came also the resurrection of the dead."

The Messiah was alive! They didn't need the spices because there was no smell of death! It was time to wave the barley, the least among the grains, and the One Who had laid aside the glory that He had with the Father to be humbly clothed in the flesh of a human was making His appearance as the Victor over death and the grave. It was the beginning of the restoration of hope!

What God in His wisdom had hidden as a mystery from mortal and demonic view was now made manifest by the Holy Spirit Who raised Christ from the dead.

The next verses in the passage give us hope when our circumstances hold none: "But as it is written, Eye has not seen, nor ear heard, neither have entered into the heart of man, the things which God has prepared for them that love Him. But God has revealed them unto us by His Spirit: for the Spirit searches all things, yea, the deep things of God" (1 Corinthians 2:9-10).

Let us look into the deeper things that God has prearranged for us. His purposes are beyond our most wonderful imaginations, but it is His pleasure to reveal them to us by His Holy Spirit.

Chapter 2

I Bore for You

A Message from the Lord from My Journal, August, 2005

When I walked the earth, every unclean thing I touched became clean because I could not be defiled. In the same way, when you bring Me your problem and you release it into My hands, the problem becomes transformed by My touch. The key is that you have to let it go from your hands into Mine. It's not a problem to Me once it becomes Mine—it becomes the building block for the solution.

It was only when I was in the Garden of Gethsemane and laid down My will in exchange for My Father's that the process appeared to change, for I had to become sin to redeem you from it [2 Corinthians 5:21].

I became "defiled." The scenario started with Judas' kiss and I bore for you treachery and betrayal. The process continued with the scattering of My beloved and trusted disciples and I bore for you abandonment. Then the guards of My own Temple arrested Me and I bore for you mutiny and treason. They bound Me and I bore for you false arrest. They handled Me roughly and I bore for you abuse.

They brought Me before Annas and I bore for you "kangaroo court," for he was not the legitimate High Priest and had no authority. They brought Me before Caiaphas and I bore for you false accusation before the religious hierarchy. I spoke the truth before Caiaphas and when the officer hit Me, I bore for you undeserved blows.

I watched while Peter swore he didn't know Me and I bore for you a loved one's denial. I truthfully admitted to being the Messiah, the Son of God, and declared they would see Me in My Majesty, and the High Priest and council of My Own People said My truth was blasphemy, and I bore for you venomous scorn, loathing, and condemnation by religious leaders.

When they threw Me into the dungeon in Caiaphas' house, I bore for you being cast into prison in innocence. I bore for you the hopelessness of being locked away and the uncertainty of what the day would bring.

They took Me to Pilate the first time, and when he sent Me to Herod, I bore for you unwillingness to get involved, even though the governor considered Me innocent. When Herod was delighted to see Me, I bore for you the disrespect of curiosity seekers. When I chose not to respond to Herod's self-indulgence and the chief priests' and scribes' vehemence, I bore for you silence in place of justified self-defense. When Herod's soldiers dealt with Me, I bore for you mocking, jeering, contempt, despising and low esteem—this at the hand of the civil guard. When they put upon My shoulders Herod's gorgeous robe, I bore for you mockery and injustice of a usurper.

When I was returned to Pilate and he declared My innocence, he offered to "teach Me a lesson" at the hand of his soldiers and release Me, and I bore for you man-pleasing chastisement in the face of My innocence. When the crowd of My People chose the seditious murderer, Barabbas, to be released instead of innocent Me, I bore for you the lot of the scapegoat. When the crowd called for

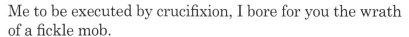

Me to be executed by crucifixion, I bore for you the wrath of a fickle mob.

When the Roman soldiers stripped Me, I bore for you shame and embarrassment. When they whipped Me with vicious devices, I bore for you undeserved punishment. When My flesh was ripped from My body and My blood flowed freely, I bore for you pain, and My healing virtue that was still on reserve—that had been released whenever I touched the sick and infirm—was released into Earth's atmosphere to be available to all. When the perverse, cruel, and sadistic men mistreated Me in every way possible, I bore for you sexual harassment, molestation, sodomy and rape. When they put the crown of thorns upon My head, I bore for you every type of head pain and mental torment. When they hit Me in the face, I bore for you disfigurement and "losing face." When they demanded that I prophesy to them, I bore for you mocking of spiritual gifts. When they cynically bowed the knee to Me, jeeringly saying "Hail, King of the Jews," I bore for you disrespect. When they spit on Me, I bore for you contempt and disdain. When I felt their anti-Semitism, I bore for you prejudice and racism.

When I was made to carry My cross, I bore for you cruelty and forcing beyond My strength. When I fell under the weight of the cross, I bore for you falling under the weight of sin. When I fell the second time, I bore for you falling into temptation over and over.

When I arrived at Golgotha, I bore for you fear of death in that place of execution. When they offered Me vinegar with gall, for you I refused to take the sedating, anaesthetising substance that you would not suffer more pain than I did. And for you I refused to receive bitterness to give you the strength to refuse it. When they drove the nails into My hands, I bore for you the destruction of My hands—My ability to work, to touch. The power to heal that was in My hands was released for you. When they drove the nails into My feet, I bore for you the destruction of My feet, My walk—My ability to go, to travel. When I spoke the words, "Father, forgive them, for they know not what they do," I bore for you the ability to forgive transgression against you.

When the soldiers parted My garments and cast lots for them, I bore for you humiliation and the spoiling of My goods. When they hung My sentence over My head, I bore for you abhorrence and derision, for My people were abhorred by Rome and they delighted in the idea that they could kill their King and throw it in the face of the religious leaders. When they placed Me between two thieves, I bore for you being surrounded and treated like a common criminal. When passersby wagged their heads at Me and taunted Me with My own words, I bore for you reviling and rejection of men. When the religious leaders scoffed at Me and ridiculed My trust in My Father, I bore for you insults and sarcasm towards faith in God and in His Word.

When I cried, "My God, My God, why have you forsaken Me?" I bore for you the feeling of abandonment by God. When one of the thieves repented, I bore for you the grace to speak kind words even under intense persecution. When the sun was darkened, I bore for you the oppression of darkness.

When I gave John to My mother and My mother to John, I bore for you the grace to make provision for loved ones even while dying. When I said, "I thirst," and received only vinegar, I bore for you unquenched thirst and all lack of provision for needs. When I said, "It is finished," I bore for you the completion of all things needed for your complete salvation, healing and total restoration of your spirit, soul and body.

When the soldier pierced My side, I bore for you wounding even after death. When the centurion declared, "Truly this was the Son of God," I bore for you the witness of the truth from your captors/persecutors. When the earth quaked, I bore for you the shaking of every foundation. When they laid Me in a borrowed tomb, I bore for you the provision of the rich.

When I stepped into the realm of the dead, I bore for you crossing Jordan without fear. When I took the keys of Hell and Death, I bore for you victory over the final enemy. When I led captivity captive, I bore for you the conquest of the enemy and set the captives free. When I rose from the dead, I bore for you resurrection life and a glorified body. When I appeared to many after My resurrection, I bore for you signs and wonders and impartation of faith to others.

So you see that while the grace seemed to be withheld from Me in the short term while I exercised My passion, it was for the purpose of releasing the greater grace for all mankind in the long term. Don't be discouraged by the short-term circumstances you see all around you. Put your trust in Me and My finished work, and rejoice in the privilege of entering into My sufferings.

Romans 8:18: For I reckon that the sufferings of this present time are not worthy to be compared with the glory which shall be revealed in us.

2 Corinthians 1:5: For as the sufferings of Christ abound in us, so our consolation also abounds by Christ.

2 Corinthians 1:6: And whether we be afflicted, it is for your consolation and salvation, which is effectual in the enduring of the same sufferings which we also suffer: or whether we be comforted, it is for your consolation and salvation.

Chapter 3

"Behold My Hands and My Feet"

"And He said unto them, Why are you troubled? and why do thoughts arise in your hearts? **Behold My hands and My feet**, that it is I myself: handle Me, and see; for a spirit has not flesh and bones, as you see Me have" (Luke 24:38-39).

After Jesus' resurrection, Mary Magdalene, Mary (the mother of James), Joanna, and Salome went to the tomb to anoint His body, but He wasn't there. They received a message of hope from angels who reminded them that Jesus had told them while they were in Galilee with Him that He would be given over to sinful men, be crucified, and rise again the third day. They were told that they should tell the good news to the disciples, so they ran to obey. In their great grief, the disciples didn't believe them. They thought the women were talking nonsense.

But Peter and John had to find out for themselves, and ran to the tomb. They viewed the linen grave clothes and napkin that had been around Jesus' face, folded in the manner that He used. Peter walked away wondering, but John walked away believing.[1]

Then Jesus appeared to Simon and Cleopas as they were walking on the road to Emmaus, but He didn't reveal His identity to them at first. Instead, He gave them a scripture lesson, opening their understanding to all that was written of Himself from the writings of Moses and the prophets. His words caused their hearts to burn within them. They persuaded Him to come and spend the night with them, and when He blessed and broke the bread at supper, their eyes were opened to recognize Him and He disappeared from their sight.

They ran back to Jerusalem to tell the disciples. While they were sharing the excitement of their experience, Jesus appeared right in the middle of them and said, "Shalom!"

The disciples were terrified and thought they were seeing a ghost! But Jesus calmly asked them why they were afraid. He invited them to touch Him, explaining that spirits don't have flesh and bones as He had. Then He showed them His hands and feet. This was proof positive that He was risen from the dead—it was really Him! And their terror turned to such overwhelming joy that they still couldn't believe it! He even demonstrated that He could eat food.

Then He opened their understanding and explained the scriptures to them about His suffering and resurrection. What had been hidden from their understanding began to make sense when they saw His wounds from Heaven's perspective as declared in the Word of God. These were mysteries to them until they were fulfilled.

From the time Jesus was crucified until He appeared to them, their hearts had been filled with fear, for they had been taunted by spiritual enemies who whispered lies

---

1   Luke 24:1-12, John 20:1-8

in their minds that they would be the next to be crucified because they had put their trust in this dead messiah. Their hopes and dreams—their whole world—had been shattered.

They hadn't been able to process what had taken place on these days when they were supposed to be celebrating the escape of their forefathers from the cruel taskmasters of Egypt. They were too close to the situation to be able to see that the sacrifice of the Passover lamb they had practiced all their lives in this first month of the year was a rehearsal for a greater event.

This magnificent Passover Lamb would fulfil the rehearsed event from Heaven's perspective. This Passover Lamb would once-and-for-all conquer the death angel, the same destroyer who had snatched away Egypt's firstborn. They hadn't been able to see that the death of THIS Passover Lamb didn't only shield them from death on the night of the Passover, He bore their sins as the atonement sacrifice, the ultimate sin offering. He removed the legal right of the accuser[2] of the brethren to press charges to condemn to death those who believed in His atoning work (Romans 6:23, "For the wages of sin is death; but the gift of God is eternal life through Jesus Christ our Lord").

The Sacrificial Lamb

According to Exodus 12:5, the "lamb" (the Hebrew word *seh*, Strong's Number H7716, meaning "one of a flock"[3]) for the Passover sacrifice could be taken from the sheep or from the goats.

Interestingly, the first mention of the Hebrew word *seh* is in Genesis 22:7 where Isaac asks his father, Abraham, "where is the lamb [*seh*] for a burnt offering?" To which Abraham replied in faith, "God will provide himself a

---

2   a legal term equivalent to a prosecuting attorney

3   https://www.blueletterbible.org/lang/lexicon/lexicon.cfm?Strongs=H7716&t=KJV

lamb [*seh*] for a burnt offering." They proceeded up Mount Moriah where Abraham was prepared to offer his own son in obedience to God's instructions to him. This was the rehearsal that linked Abraham, the father of our faith, with the long-range purposes of our Heavenly Father.

Abraham was stopped by the Lord as he took up the knife to slay his son as a sacrifice, and God provided a ram for a substitute. Abraham was God's friend and He included him in the revelation on the earth of what He would do to His own Son, making Him a substitute sacrifice on that same mountain.

This was the place Abraham named "Yehovah Yireh" (Jehovah Jirah), literally "Yehovah sees the need and sees to it."[4] Abraham named the place prophetically for what would come there.

It's the place of Araunah's threshing floor. This was the place the angel of judgment was stopped after he had slain 70,000 when the Lord's anger was kindled against Israel and He moved David to number the people. David purchased the place, built an altar, and offered burnt offerings and peace offerings. The Lord was appeased and stopped the plague.

---

4   The thought is very close to the definition of the Greek word for God's love, *agapé*, "...benevolent love. Its benevolence, however, is not shown by doing what the person loved desires but what the one who loves deems as needed by the one loved (e.g., For God so loved [*ēgápēsen*] the world that He gave...John 3:16). He gave not what man wanted, but what man needed as God perceived his need, namely His Son who brought forgiveness to man. God's love for man is His doing what He thinks best for man and not what man desires..."

"Agapé" Strong's G25 definition from "Lexical Aids to the New Testament" by Spiros Zodhiates, *Hebrew Greek Key Study Bible*, (c) 1984 and 1991 Spiros Zodhiates and AMG International, Inc. Chattanooga, TN.

This was the place David prepared for Solomon to build the Temple. He used the part of the mountain directly north of the City of David for it. Psalm 48:1-2 refers to it as Mount Zion, beautifully situated on the northern slope.

When the Temple was dedicated, the fire came down from Heaven and consumed the burnt offerings and sacrifices,[5] and the Shekinah Glory came as a cloud so that the priests weren't able to stand. The Lord was pleased to have this place as His "House of Sacrifice."[6] This was the place He chose for offerings to be made to appease Him for sin. Every year multitudes of *sehs* were offered on Mount Moriah.

Even the Antonia Fortress was on Mount Moriah. This was where Jesus was scourged in fufilment of Isaiah 53. He became the Suffering Servant who "was wounded for our transgressions and bruised for our iniquities: the chastisement of our peace was upon Him; and with His stripes we are healed. All we like sheep have gone astray; we have turned every one to his own way; and the Lord has laid on Him the iniquity of us all. He was oppressed, and He was afflicted, yet He opened not His mouth: He is brought as a lamb [*seh*] to the slaughter, and as a sheep before her shearers is dumb, so He opens not His mouth... Yet it pleased the Lord to bruise Him; He has put Him to grief: when you shalt make His soul an offering for sin, He shall see His seed, He shall prolong His days, and the pleasure of the Lord shall prosper in His hand. He shall see of the travail of His soul, and shall be satisfied: by His knowledge shall My righteous servant justify many; for He shall bear their iniquities. Therefore will I divide Him a portion with the great, and He shall divide the spoil with the strong; because He has poured out His soul unto death: and He was numbered with the transgressors; and

---

5   2 Chronicles 7:1-3

6   2 Chronicles 7:12

He bare the sin of many, and made intercession for the transgressors" (verses 5-7, 10-12).

Further north, beyond the site of the Temple, was the place where Solomon's workers had quarried out the stones to build it. The quarry later became a place of execution. The Romans used it for crucifixion. Here the unblemished *seh*, the sinless Yeshua (Saviour) was sacrificed on a cruel Roman cross.

Jesus was the *seh* on broken remains of ancient Mount Moriah at the same time that the priests were slaughtering Passover lambs in the Temple. But He was more than just the Passover Lamb.

When God gave instructions in Numbers 28 for the various daily sacrifices, He specified that in the celebration of the Feast of the Passover, they were to bring "one goat for a sin offering, to make an atonement for you" (verse 22). Jesus was the goat for the sin offering as well, to make an atonement for us.

The definition of "atonement" from the online *Oxford English Dictionary* is:

1 The action of making amends for a wrong or injury.

1.1 (in religious contexts) reparation or expiation for sin.

1.2 (the Atonement) Christian Theology The reconciliation of God and mankind through Jesus Christ.

Origin

Early 16th century (denoting unity or reconciliation, especially between God and man): from at one + -ment, influenced by medieval Latin *adunamentum* 'unity,' and earlier onement from an obsolete verb one 'to unite.'[7]

The Merriam-Webster Dictionary online describes the etymology (word origin) of atone: "Atone comes to us from the combination in Middle English of at and on, the latter of which is an old variant of one. Together they meant 'in harmony.' (In current English, we use at one with a similar suggestion of harmony in such phrases as "at one with nature.") When it first entered English, atone meant "to reconcile and suggested the restoration of a peaceful and harmonious state between people or groups." These days the verb specifically implies addressing the damage (or disharmony) caused by one's own behavior." [8]

Strong's Definitions gives us a deeper look. "H3722 *kâphar*, [pronounced] kaw-far'; ... to cover (specifically with bitumen); figuratively, to expiate or condone, to placate or cancel:—appease, make (an atonement, cleanse, disannul, forgive, be merciful, pacify, pardon, purge (away), put off, (make) reconcile(-liation)."[9]

The first mention of the Hebrew word *kâphar* in scripture is in Genesis 6:14 where God instructs Noah to cover the ark inside and outside with pitch (bitumen). This black, tarry substance made the ark waterproof, enabling it to ride upon the surface of the flood of judgment on the sins of mankind. In the same way, the atonement sacrifice each year on Yom Kippur covered the sins of the nation of Israel so that God's judgment on sin (death) would be appeased.

---

7   "atonement, n. 1." *Oxford English Dictionary* Online. June 2019. Oxford University Press. https://en.oxforddictionaries.com/definition/atonement (accessed 8 June, 2019) © 2019

8   "atone." *Merriam-Webster.com*. 2019 https://www.merriam-webster.com/dictionary/atone#etymology (accessed 08 June 2019).

9   *Blue Letter Bible*. 2019. https://www.blueletterbible.org/lang/lexicon/lexicon.cfm?Strongs=H3722&t=KJV. (accessed 08 June 2019).

But the glorious sacrifice of Jesus as the ultimate Passover Lamb and atonement sin offering covers us inside and out with His glorious sinlessness when we surrender to Him as our Lord and Saviour. He "dwells in our hearts by faith"[10] (inside) and when we are baptized into Christ/the Messiah, we put on Christ/the Messiah[11] (outside), making us complete in Him![12] That lifts us up above the flood of judgment, even better than Noah's ark!

When Jesus first appeared to the disciples after His resurrection and showed them His hands and His feet, it was just the beginning of revelation. For that moment it was enough for them to realize that He was raised from the dead. Even then they couldn't really believe it!

Our Father's plan had been hidden from them. But, like Joseph who had been sold into Egypt by his brothers, that which had all appearances of evil was part of a greater plan to bring salvation and redemption to the whole house of Israel and the nations.

---

10   Ephesians 3:17

11   Galatians 3:27

12   Colossians 3:10

Chapter 4

From Heaven's Perspective

"For as the heavens are higher than the earth, so are My ways higher than your ways, and My thoughts than your thoughts" (Isaiah 55:9).

So how high are the heavens? Louis Giglio did a fantastic job of demonstrating the greatness of our Creator in his video presentation, "Indescribable."[1]

Here are a few facts from his message:

- The distances in space are so vast that they must be measured by the speed of light (186,000 miles per second—that's seven and a half times around the earth at the equator per second) travelling for a year, that is one light year. In other words, a light year is the measuring stick that's used to show expanses in the universe, and it is 5.88 trillion miles long!

- Scientists estimate that there are billions of stars in our galaxy, the Milky Way.

---

1   Louie Giglio Passion Update _ Indescribable (Dec 04, 2017). Louis Giglio Sermons. https://www.youtube.com/watch?v=vo88XK8BQaE

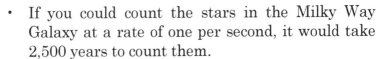

- If you could count the stars in the Milky Way Galaxy at a rate of one per second, it would take 2,500 years to count them.

- If you could travel at the speed of light (186,000 miles per second), it would take you 100,000 years to cross the Milky Way Galaxy. [Known history from the Garden of Eden until now is only approximately 6,000 years.]

- Scientists estimate that there are hundreds of billions of galaxies in the known universe, and that every second a new star is being born.

Isaiah 40:12 indicates that God measures the heavens with the span of His hand—that's the distance between His thumb and little finger! So how big is our Creator? We can't begin to imagine that. The concept is too vast! It takes the entire universe to declare His glory.[2]

So if man is completely incapable of measuring what God can measure with His hand, ponder for a moment how much higher His ways are than our ways!

"Yet It Pleased the Lord to Bruise Him..."[3]

Isaiah 53 is such a clear picture of Jesus' sufferings for our forgiveness of sin, our physical, emotional, and mental healing, the restoration of our relationship with our Father, and more. It's easy for us to see in hindsight from the 21st century, especially if we have "evangelical glasses." Unless the Lord gave Isaiah a vision from which to write that prophecy, he would have been clueless. To the disciples it was a mystery until Jesus revealed it to them.

Most of us get it that Jesus was our substitutional sacrifice, but it's still hard to wrap our minds around the

---

2   Psalm 19:1

3   Isaiah 53:10

concept that it actually "**pleased the Lord to bruise Him.**" That was His Son—His only begotten Son! How could our loving Father do that? The rejection, the injustice, the torture, the agony, the pain—it's nearly incomprehensible to our minds that this could possibly please God! But the scripture clearly says that it did.

If we could look back in time before our Creator said, "Let there be light,"[4] we can imagine that He looked forward through what we, looking back, call history. He foresaw all of the generations and individuals that ever would be. He planned the part that each of us would play in history, placing a destiny in our DNA. He gave each of us gifts to share to make Him known. He foresaw all of our flaws, all of the choices we would ever make—the good, the bad, and the stupid. But knowing ahead of time that we would turn and repent, He planned and orchestrated out there ahead of us how it would all work together for our good.[5]

He foresaw the sin of Adam and Eve that would plunge the earth into degradation, twisting and warping what God had made perfect. He foresaw our need of a Saviour, and so it was determined from the foundation of the world that the Lamb was slain to correct the chaos.

Clearly, redemption pleases our Father!

Revealed by the Holy Spirit

"**But as it is written, Eye has not seen, nor ear heard, neither have entered into the heart of man, the things which God has prepared for them that love Him. But God has revealed them unto us by His Spirit: for the Spirit searches all things, yea, the deep things of God**" (1 Corinthians 2:9-10).

4   Genesis 1:3

5   Romans 8:28

Our vastly Almighty God, Creator and King of the Universe, has hidden many mysteries—many "deep things"— in His heart that He reveals by His Spirit. When those who love Him seek Him with all their heart and soul, He promises that they will find Him.[6]

Moses Asks a Favour

When the Children of Israel had thoroughly disgusted the Lord with their partying before a golden calf idol, He declared to Moses that He refused to go with them into the Promised Land, warning them that He would likely rise up in the middle of them and consume them all. He sent them to their tents to let Him ponder what to do.[7]

The Lord knew that He could trust Moses, and spoke with him face to face with grace and favour. In Exodus 33:13, Moses interceded, "Now therefore, I pray you, if I have found grace in your sight, **shew me now Your way, that I may know You,** that I may find grace in your sight: and consider that this nation is your people." Moses continued and the Lord relented due to his intercession. Then Moses asked one more favour in verse 18: "**I beseech You, shew me Your glory.**"

"And He said, **I will make all My goodness pass before you,** and I will proclaim the name of the Lord before you; and will be gracious to whom I will be gracious, and will shew mercy on whom I will shew mercy. And He said, You cannot see My face: for there shall no man see Me, and live. And the Lord said, Behold, there is a place by Me, and you shalt stand upon a rock: And it shall come to pass, while My glory pass by, that I will put you in a cleft of the rock, and will cover you with My hand while I pass by: And I will take away mine hand, **and you shalt see**

6   Deuteronomy 4:29, Hebrews 11:6

7   Exodus 32:35-33:5

My back parts: but My face shall not be seen" (Exodus 33:19-23).

Moses wanted the Lord to:

* show him His way
* let him know Him
* show him His glory

These requests certainly pleased our Father! He instructed Moses to go up Mount Sinai for this experience. When He came down in the Cloud of His Presence and passed by Moses, He roared His name twice, then began describing His character and intent to Moses. As He did, He showed Moses His Way—that is, His back—mutilated with the stripes He had borne since the foundation of the world. It was surely the greatest Glory, hidden from mankind, and hidden from the adversary. This was the glorious mystery that would go beyond the stone tablets of His code of conduct to release into the earth through those terrible wounds the grace to be able to follow Him through loving Him.

Moses quickly bowed and worshipped, saying, "If now I have found grace in your sight, O Lord, let my Lord, I pray you, go among us; for it is a stiff-necked people; and **pardon our iniquity and our sin**, and take us for your inheritance" (Exodus 34:9).

Moses had seen the glorious provision of Yeshua, Jesus, **the Way**, the Truth, and the Life, whose back was wounded for our transgressions and bruised for our iniquities! He was given the revelation of the path to know God, even before it was manifested in the earth! He was permitted to see the Glory of the Plan of salvation from the foundation of the earth!

Before Moses even rolled out to the people all the details of the tabernacle, the sacrifices, and all the minutia of the law, he saw that these things were a pattern that would be fulfilled by "that prophet" that Moses told the people would come after him.[8] This was a part of the pattern shown him in the mount.[9]

Jesus' Glorification

As Jesus is coming to the end of His earthly ministry, He begins to talk about His "glorification." Remember what Moses saw when He requested to see the Lord's glory.

> And Jesus [said], The hour is come, that the Son of man should be **glorified**. Verily, verily, I say unto you, Except a corn of wheat fall into the ground and **die**, it abides alone: but **if it die, it brings forth much fruit**. He that loves his life shall lose it; and he that hates his life in this world shall keep it unto life eternal. If any man serve Me, let him follow Me; and where I am, there shall also My servant be: if any man serve Me, him will My Father honour. Now is My soul troubled; and what shall I say? Father, save me from this hour: **but for this cause came I unto this hour. Father, glorify Your name**. Then came there a voice from heaven, saying, **I have both glorified it, and will glorify it again**. The people therefore, that stood by, and heard it, said that it thundered: others said, An angel spoke to him. Jesus answered and said, This voice came not because of Me, but for your sakes. Now is the judgment of this world: now shall the prince of this world be cast out. **And I, if I be lifted up from the earth, will draw all men unto me. This he said, signifying what death he should die.** (John 12:23-33).

Then just days later, after the Passover meal:

---

8   Deuteronomy 18:15-18

9   Hebrews 8:5

Jesus... was troubled in spirit, and testified, and said, Verily, verily, I say unto you, that **one of you shall betray Me**.... He then lying on Jesus' breast said to Him, Lord, who is it? Jesus answered, He it is, to whom I shall give a sop, when I have dipped it. And when he had dipped the sop, he gave it to Judas Iscariot, the son of Simon. And after the sop satan entered into him. Then said Jesus unto him, That you do, do quickly.... He then having received the sop went immediately out: and it was night. Therefore, when he was gone out, Jesus said, **Now is the Son of man glorified, and God is glorified in him. If God be glorified in him, God shall also glorify him in himself, and shall straightway glorify him.** (John 13:21, 25-27, 30-32).

When we think about glorification, we think about the resurrection, but we don't tend to think about the path that led there. Jesus went to the Garden of Gethsemane and agonized in travailing, groaning prayer in such agony that it caused Him to "sweat great drops of blood" (Luke 22:44). When He had prayed through there, His betrayer appeared and identified Him to the temple guards who arrested Him. He was roughly led to Caiaphas where one of His closest companions denied even knowing Him, and even cursed in the midst of his denial. He passed through trial after trial with lying witnesses and unjust judges. He endured mocking, being pierced in the head by a crown of thorns, having his beard pulled out, whipping with multiple strands that were tipped with bone or metal, designed to tear the flesh.

He endured every type of indignity—anything humans have suffered or will, He suffered. He was forced to carry a cross through the jeering crowds in the streets of Jerusalem, and then was nailed to it, between two thieves. Jesus suffered the long, agonizing death by asphyxiation that many consider to be the cruelest form of execution ever devised by demonically-inspired mankind.

This was the path to Jesus' glorification. It began when Judas walked out into the night to make the deal to betray Him. We don't think in terms of anything so horrific, painful, and shameful as being very glorious, but from Heaven's point of view, that's exactly what it was!

Visions of the Wounds

Vision 1

Many people have had visions of the wounds of Jesus. My friend, Marylois Little, tells of how she saw Jesus on the cross. As she looked up at Him in all His suffering, His blood dripped down on her. In His agony He formed the words, "I love you!" Each word was separated as blood dropped from His mouth, with great effort to say, "I — love — you." She was overwhelmed.

Vision 2

Oden Hetrick, in his book, *Inside the Gates of Heaven,* relates an incident on his first visit to Heaven:

I was again standing by my Savior, close to His left hand. I was made to understand that I was slow of heart to believe all the reality of what had been revealed to me. Then the unifying Spirit of God who controls all actions in that land caused me to take Jesus' left hand and turn the palm toward me. My soul failed as I looked at the scar that doubting Thomas also saw after he said, "Except I see the print of the nails in His hands, I shall not believe." The scar, that I thought was only a little hole, was a healed tear from the base of His thumb to His two center fingers. There I saw the evidence of the precious price paid for mankind by love untold. As I beheld my Redeemer's hand, I was told, Now you must believe. I could not restrain the tears of sorrow as I looked at the scar and realized that Jesus had to die for my sins. But thankfulness brought tears of joy because He did, and because He redeemed me, loves me, gives me visions, helps me understand heavenly love, and because He has prepared for me a place of perfect habitation.

Vision 3

Oden Hetrick's daughter, Joyful Star, also has visions of Heaven. Here is one account:

One time, in my chamber mansion garden where I meet with Yeshua, I was sitting at His feet, looking up at His lovely, smiling face. Wanting to express my love to Him I bent down to kiss His feet. As I did I noticed a scar on the top of one of His feet, and knew immediately what it was. It didn't look like just a hole, it looked more like a small line where the skin was broken. With tears of sadness for His suffering, and yet tears of gratitude, I kissed it tenderly, laid my hand on it and looked again at His face. He smiled and held out His hand, inviting me to sit on His lap.

Vision 4

Bert Crevier had a vision of when Moses went up to Mount Sinai and talked with the Lord:

Moses saw God walk by and he saw the scars on the Lord's back. He saw Jesus Christ in God on Mount Sinai and he saw His nail scars on His feet and His hands—all the whippings He took at Calvary.

I believe this was a prequel, the story before Jesus came to Calvary, because in the mind of Christ Jesus He had already died on the cross (AT

CALVARY). It was finished before it had begun. Hebrews chapter 12 refers to Moses' experience: When Moses saw Jesus on Mount Sinai, the sight was so terrible that he said, "I'm full of fear and trembling." So what Moses saw was JESUS CHRIST the Savior on GOD ALMIGHTY. The description of the scene on Mount Sinai in verse 18 is that it "burned with fire," and there was "blackness, and darkness, and tempest." The word "tempest" means "THUNDER AND LIGHTNING AND STORMS." THIS IS what it is like in GOD'S Presence.

Annie's Visions

Annie Schisler, a well-known actress in Argentina, came to the Lord during a tremendous revival in the late 1960s. Knowing no doctrines of the faith and virtually nothing of the Bible, she began having many, many amazing visions from the Lord. She shared them with her pastor, R. Edward Miller, who translated them; they filled four books. Many of the hidden workings of God in the invisible beyond the limits of time and sense are revealed. Here are a few of her accounts of the wounds of Jesus:

Vision 5

....This time Jesus revealed Himself in a manner a little closer to human and His form was less impressive, that is to say less brilliant, less show of power yet withal very beautiful, tender, sweet and loving. The marks of the wounds of His passion were clearly visible which they always were and He wore them as if proud of them. They appeared to me cruel and ugly but He was not ashamed of them, as if they were a joy to Him.[10]

---

10   Annie Schisler. *I Looked and I Saw the Lord.* https://revivalcarriers.org/free-downloadable-ebooks-by-r-edward-miller/free-ebook-i-saw-the-lord/ 14-15 (accessed 10

Vision 6: The Vision of the Cross

When I went into prayer on the 24th of June with a special request on my heart, I was suddenly in the Spirit as at other times. But this time in much fear and anguish of spirit, for my pastor had suggested that I ask the Lord to show me His cross. I was afraid that it would be asking too much and that He would be displeased and not answer me. But Jesus said, "This request is from Me because I have desired to show you these things." Although I was both ashamed and afraid at these words, He calmed my fears and told me to look.

At first I found myself weeping greatly and pained, feeling the sensation of death about me. I had the inner sense and knowledge that I had been transported back in time to the time of the crucifixion. I felt the anguish and pain and sensed that I was actually participating in that very happening of His death, as if I, too, were dying in deep, intense pain though not in the physical. Rather as though it were a terrible pain of love. He was there before me with all of His angels and I wept much for I felt in that moment much agony. Neither could I look at either Him or at them.

Second, being in this agony, I saw before me His body all destroyed and terribly mutilated. His heart was exposed before my eyes with His side a gaping wound. The part of Him most terribly and horribly wounded was His heart. So tortured. So destroyed. So mutilated. Yet it was still beating. His body was not upon the cross but laid out before me. With all these terrible wounds His heart was still beating.

June 2019). Used by permission.

I saw that His heart greatly overflowed with mighty love that was far beyond words to tell. I could see this mighty love flowing and flowing forth from that horribly wounded heart. I felt that this love and this terrible suffering became fully identified with my own person or being. This love was tremendous, powerful and intense, passing by far the ability of even understanding it. As I beheld and was identified with Him feeling the keen pain and deep sorrow of it all, I saw His heart suddenly stop beating. This Beautiful Being died. This tremendous love stopped flowing. This being so loving and so filled with love was no more. This caused to exist in my inner being an exceeding pain, perturbation and grief. I seemed to die with Him. And now the stopping of that heart deeply perturbed me. All that love stopped flowing and it seemed that all the world stopped with it. Never in all my whole life, not even when I tried suicide, had I felt such pain and deep anguish. Agony! Pain! Horror! Anguish of spirit! All seemed to be over.

Then suddenly I found myself in a third scene. Someone said that I need not feel this pain and desperation any longer because He was with me. Suddenly He was there before me glorious and alive and strong. He drew near to me and as He drew near all the anguish and pain left. I felt as if His glorious being seemed to settle down over me and cover me with His love. Joy deep, strange and glorious filled me to overflowing, filling all the place of anguish and pain. There returned to me all the full, deep security that He lived. Peace flowed forth from His glorious Presence. He spoke to me saying that never more would I feel the pain of death. Never again would I have to pass through death as this time. I knew then that I had been identified with Him in His death, so was I now identified with Him in His life. That wonderful heart of love over which I had so grieved was now alive and would never die again.[11]

Vision 7: All About Jesus

I was again permitted to enter into the Spirit, and I found myself with Jesus and all of His angels. His love covered me as ever and this time He showed me directly, His wounds. Oh, they were so terrible. But even though they were great, ugly, painful wounds, they SHONE FORTH RAYS OF LIGHT like living jewels in His hands and feet. He showed me them as if they were His glory and His pleasure, not His shame or His pain. And the love in me for Him was so great, it was like great pain.[12]

Vision 8: Scene on a Screen

On this day, August 20, I found it very hard to enter into His Presence in prayer. I was in much desperation of spirit and in many tears. Suddenly, I found myself in the Spirit. There was Jesus in all His usual beauty and splendor and the angels with Him. Immediately, all the sense of desperation left and there flooded my being that tremendous love and peace that He ever radiates upon me. All welcomed me with such tender looks and sweet smiles. But right away Jesus spoke to me, telling me to look. As I did so, I saw as it were, a large screen before me like a window into another world. The angels with me also turned to look at the scene so strangely portrayed before me. In that scene,

---

11   Ibid. 16-17.

12   Ibid. 20.

I saw Christ seated upon a throne. Around Him were many angels.

But how strange it was! For this Christ that I saw before me was a manifestation so vastly different from the One who stood beside me and bade me look. There He was so high, so filled with glory and splendor and so vastly increased in size and majesty. All the angels standing around Him also were of a type of beings I had never before seen. Because they were distinctly different in their whole beings and vastly much brighter and greater in size, I knew immediately that they were of an order of angelic beings much superior to those seen hitherto and to those who were with me looking at this portrayal or manifestation. They were so much more beautiful and perfect in their harmonious beings, yet they radiated tenderness, love and great kindness. This Christ so glorious and beautiful, so far, far superior to those glorious beings surrounding Him, allowed me to see His wounds. Oh, how different they were! He wore them as blazing jewels. They shined forth in beautiful rays and He wore them like beautiful adornments of His Person. This Christ was so mighty, brilliant and awesome that I was filled with dread. But the Jesus who stood beside me and showed me this manifestation of His greater self in majesty and power spoke to me telling me not to fear. Then this fear left me.[13]

Vision 9

Jesus allowed me once again to see His wounds, but they were not like the ugly wounds seen on Him in the inferior plane. They were like most glorious jewels or lustrous gems that He gloried

13   Ibid, 22-23.

in. He, Himself, was tremendously bright with celestial light that far outshines our poor little sun. So sublime, so huge in size, sending forth great rays of purest light, He was so high I could not draw very near unto Him. He spoke to me telling me that I could not draw very near to Him because I could neither resist nor endure to be any nearer in my present state. He also said, "You may see Me and you shall not fear. It is being prepared for you to be able to come up higher." Then He spoke again saying that my lack of feeling the sweetness and tenderness in His love was because His love was now too great and powerful, and that I could not comprehend His love for me because it was far too great for my limited ability to understand. He said that if He would make His love very small and reduce it to the smallest size, then I could feel it and receive it in a manner that would satisfy my longing, for I had not yet been given the faculties to be able to understand His higher love.[14]

Vision 10

Christ, reigning in great power, was tremendously glorious. His person appeared to be like gold filled with fire, refulgent and radiating light in intense brilliancy. His eyes were very penetrating and like blazing fires from which reflected powerful rays. There proceeded from Him much, much love. It seemed to radiate from His hands, His feet and from His whole body. His whole person was as a halo of most refulgent glory-light. His wounds scintillated from the beauty of their brilliancy. Oh, He was so glorious, so beautiful and so high that His glory seemed to fill all of space.[15]

---

14 Ibid, 30-31.

15 Ibid, 33.

Vision 11

All around the head of Christ were most intense, brilliant lights as if they were a crown. It looked as if it might have been the marks of the wounds made by His crown of thorns, though of this I could not be certain. This crown of lights was like bright, lighted, living diamonds which circled His head and was most similar to the jewel-like lights of His other wounds of which I could be more sure.[16]

Vision 12 The Weapons of Jesus

It was the afternoon of the fourth of September that I found much opposition to entering into His Presence in prayer. There was much inner distraction. Opposing negative thoughts bothered me. But as I pressed on in prayer, I was suddenly there in the spirit realms. Jesus was there before me and this time there were a number of those perfect ones who are always with Him. I saw Him with great clarity and He was most lovely. That which was most outstanding were the brilliant lights that were round about His head which seemed to actually be a part of Him. They were very brilliant and shone forth in many most beautiful rays of purest celestial light, so different from our light that it seemed to have substance also.

His body of burning, blazing gold was like the clearest, purest crystal. All of His wounds from His passion shone with exceeding brilliancy and beauty. Oh, such beauty is impossible to convey and it hurts me to even try for I seem to bungle and spoil it even to try to describe it.[17]

16   Ibid. 33-34.

17   Ibid. 41.

Why So Different?

So why do the different accounts not agree in their details? Remember, God's ways are higher than our ways. He made each of us unique, and He addresses our situation and level of maturity uniquely. Annie Schisler saw Jesus in several different forms, and each vision had a different lesson for her to learn.

John the Beloved saw Jesus in various forms in the book of Revelation. He saw Him walking in Glory among the seven lampstands, having white hair, fiery eyes, feet like burnished bronze, and a sword coming out of His mouth. His countenance was as bright as the sun.[18] Later he saw Him as the slain Lamb with seven horns and seven eyes.[19] In chapter 14, he saw Him sitting on a cloud with a golden crown on His head and a sharp sickle in His hand.[20] Finally, John saw Him coming on a white horse. His eyes were flaming, and He had many crowns on His head. His robe was dipped in blood, and a sharp sword came out of His mouth. On His robe and on His thigh were written the words, "King of kings and Lord of lords.[21]

Sometimes we need to see Jesus in His earthly form, and sometimes we need to see Him as the amazing, glorified Messiah that is bright and blinding. He always is to us what we need Him to be, and He knows best what that is, whether the Slain Lamb or the Lion of the Tribe of Judah. Sometimes we need to see His wounds as raw and bloody, and sometimes we need to see them as resplendent and rich like jewels worn by the Conqueror of Death, Hell, and the Grave.

---

18   Revelation 1:13-16.

19   Ibid. 5:6.

20   Ibid. 14:14.

21   Ibid. 19:11-16.

Chapter 5

Our Beginnings

"Before I formed you in the belly I knew you; and before you came forth out of the womb I sanctified you, and I ordained you a prophet unto the nations" (Jeremiah 1:5).

"You formed my innermost being, shaping my delicate inside and my intricate outside, and wove them all together in my mother's womb... You even formed every bone in my body when You created me in the secret place, carefully, skillfully shaping me from nothing to something. You saw who You created me to be before I became me! Before I'd ever seen the light of day, the number of days you planned for me were already recorded in Your book" (Psalm 139:13, 15-16 TPT).

The Holy Spirit reveals in these passages that our Father had a plan for each of us before we were even conceived. Surely His plan was for us to be victorious overcomers, coming to earth to help Him restore His Kingdom based on the finished work of the Lord Jesus on the cross. From the beginning, His goal has been to see the day described in Revelation 7:9-10. "After this I beheld, and, lo, a great multitude, which no man could number, of **all nations, and kindreds, and people, and tongues,** stood before the throne, and before the Lamb, clothed with white robes, and palms in their hands; And cried with a loud voice, saying, Salvation to our God which sits upon the throne, and unto the Lamb."

It is God's will for "all to be saved, and to come unto the knowledge of the truth."[1] He put it deeply into our spirit that we relate to Him and be a part of His Plan for the earth.

Patrick Holloran, a seer and apostolic, prophetic teacher, had a tremendous revelation that he included in his book, *Foundations of the Supernatural Lifestyle.*

He could see that a guardian angel comes to protect a child at conception in its mother's womb, and continues to stand guard over the infant after birth.

When his children were born, he could see in the spirit realm that there was an event that took place that he called a "presentation ceremony." The angels that would serve that child at various times in his/her life came "to be introduced to the supernatural destiny of the baby." He noticed that in addition to the angels, "a demonic scribe who was carrying a perverted book of remembrance" would attend. "His mission was to find out what the angels were bringing in the time of introduction. He would then record it and place it in a library of information that the enemy [the forever loser] keeps.... What the demonic pursues is the opposite of what God stands for.... The enemy will then seek out any generational curses/iniquities that are in an individual's family line."

As Pat grew spiritually, he asked the Lord that in the day of his "grandchildren being born that there would be no ability of the enemy to learn their gifting, calling, and mantles." He wrote:

---

1   1 Timothy 2:4

When my oldest grandchild was born, I started to pray for protection for her. I prayed over the birthing room, established a Canopy of Protection, and even took the table of the Lord. We were, as a family, getting ready to pray over her and dedicate her to God in the name of Jesus Christ. In an instant there came into the room several angelic warrior servants who took positions along the walls. They each looked at my grandchild, then they turned outward. As they did this, they locked their shields together to form a perimeter guard in the room. After this establishing of a defensive position, the other angels that would be involved in my grandchild's life arrived and presented themselves.

As I was watching this, two of the angelic warriors parted their shields momentarily. When I looked through the gap, I discovered that outside the window, not twenty feet away, was a demonic scribe, trying to look inside the room. He had with him a writing tool and a book. As I saw the name on the book being that of my granddaughter, I spoke out, "No!" Then before I could say anything else, another angel of war came and literally snatched that scribe away. As the book and writing tool were still in the air, fire came from above and consumed both of these objects. Then the two angels standing guard on that side of the room reconnected their shields to form a solid protective wall again.[2]

Exposing Enemy Objectives

The forever loser understands that in order to keep us from reaching God's objective for our lives, his schemes have to start as early as possible. A child is designed by

---

2   Pat Holloran, *Foundations of the Supernatural Lifestyle* (Palm Harbor: Harvest House International Ministries, 2011), 75-78.

God to be like a sponge, absorbing and learning from his/ her parents.

Fathers are enjoined by Moses to teach the words of the Lord to their children when they sit together in the house, when they walk, when they lie down, and when they get up.[3] The Apostle Paul tells fathers not to provoke their children to anger, but to nurture and discipline them.[4] And God put mothering instincts in women to nurture, comfort, and nourish their children.

God designed a child to be raised in a safe, loving environment. "Infants perceive life through an emotional grid—not a logical one. So what a child most needs at this stage is his parent's loving and attentive care."[5] Under those circumstances, the child feels loved and wanted, and as an infant learns to trust that when he's hungry, he'll get fed, when she needs a diaper change, she'll get one, etc. "When caregivers are consistently unavailable, a child learns to avoid trusting others. When caregivers are consistently unreliable, a child can grow to be deeply insecure."[6]

Sadly, however, very few children get 100% of the love, nurture, healthy instruction, and appropriate correction that they need, and the results can be disastrous. Wounded children tend to grow into adults with issues, and many times those adults have no clue why.

What typically happens as a result of childhood wounding is that the emotional development of the child is arrested at that point. Although natural physical growth takes place, even adults—when triggered—will behave at

---

3   Deuteronomy 11:19

4   Ephesians 6:4

5   https://gospelcenteredfamily.com/blog/growing-to-trust-reflections-on (accessed 19 June 2019).

6   Ibid.

the age at which they were traumatized.[7] It's a setup by the forever loser to arrest children, imprison them in lies, and thus prevent them from reaching their destiny.

Many volumes have been written about rejection. It seems to be an overarching tactic used to destroy a soul. It prevents us from seeing who our Father really meant us to be. It can begin in the womb when a child hears words that are anything less than love and acceptance. Arguing, anger, physical or emotional abuse between the parents or others speaking to the mother gives rejection a kickstart in a child. Perhaps the circumstances in the timing or fathering of the child were less than perfect. This causes rejection to begin to operate even before birth.

Rejection can come as heavy blows, or like a dripping faucet. Perceived abandonment is as real to a child as actual abandonment. Normally, a child is bonded to his/her mother as the source of life and safety. When Mommy disappears from their sight, little ones can't comprehend why, because they live in the moment.

Negligence, or a lack of physical touching, can produce feelings of rejection. Insults, sarcasm, and criticism (even constructive), cause feelings of rejection. A parent or significant adult with a perfectionist attitude doesn't compliment a child's best effort if it falls short of perfection. So the child begins to feel like a failure without hope of reaching the standard of approval.

Sexual molestation is devastating to a child. **Incest** is even worse because it involves a family member. God wired us to be safe in the family environment. Because a child cannot see the "big picture" yet, demonic whispers build their perception that it's somehow their fault. They cannot perceive themselves as innocent, so they carry a weight of false responsibility. Because they feel they

7   https://childhoodtraumarecovery.com/borderline-personality-disorder-articles/
arrested-psychological-development-and-age-regression/ (accessed 19 June 2019).

deserved the abuse, they begin a life of victimization, choosing the wrong relationships.

Emotional abuse (such as abandonment, cutting words, neglect, humiliation, screaming, threatening to deprive necessities, etc.) and **physical abuse** (such as excessive, violent corporal punishment, kicking, slapping, preventing eating, tying to a chair, locking in a closet, etc.) also take a heavy toll on a child.[8]

Any or all of these traumas will cause the child's perceptions to be warped. What we perceive is what we believe, and that builds the core of our soul. This is where the serpent whispers lies to the mind of the child that isn't capable of true reasoning.

As the accuser of the brethren, the forever loser lies to us about ourselves, about the people all around us, and about our Father. When we've been wounded, we are more susceptible to false reasoning and to getting snared into deception. Believing all these lies sets up a child to fail in his/her God-given purpose and destiny. Wounded, broken children grow up to be wounded, broken adults who go on to wound and break their children, thus perpetuating iniquity and generational curses.

Jesus' Perspective on Children

At that time the disciples came to ask Jesus, "Who is considered to be the greatest in heaven's kingdom realm?"

Jesus called a little one to His side and said to them, "Learn this well: Unless you dramatically change your way of thinking and become teachable, and learn about heaven's kingdom realm with the wide-eyed wonder of a child, you will never be able

---

8   Studies have shown that military veterans who have sought treatment for PTSD frequently had a history of abuse in childhood. https://ajp.psychiatryonline.org/doi/abs/10.1176/ajp.150.2.235 (accessed 19 June 2019).

to enter in. Whoever continually humbles himself to become like this gentle child is the greatest one in heaven's kingdom realm. And if you tenderly care for this little one on my behalf, you are tenderly caring for me. **But if anyone abuses one of these little ones who believe in Me, it would be better for him to have a heavy boulder tied around his neck and be hurled into the deepest sea than to face the punishment he deserves!** (Matthew 18:1-6).[9]

Jesus was teaching us that we are to be **childlike**. But the forever loser is busy wounding us so that we will be **childish**, even as adults.

The warning of the Lord here is to the abuser. If you were abused, the abuse must stop with you so that you don't become an abuser. Go back to chapter 2 and let the truth of all that Jesus accomplished in His passion for us permeate your being and heal you so that you can be restored and share that restoration with others. God can certainly fix us when we let His Holy Spirit teach us!

We understand that evil spirits look for entrance ways into our lives and that they use deception to cause us to open doors to them. The Word of God, the Blood of Jesus Christ, the authority of His name, and the agreement of our personal will shuts those doors, and gives us the victory that Jesus paid for. Sometimes people need extra help getting that victory. If you need Biblical counselling (the only kind we recommend), or deliverance, ask the Holy Spirit to lead you to the right person whom He has appointed to help you. He is faithful and will surely see to it.

---

9   Brian Simmons, The Passion Translation (https://www.biblegateway.com/passage/?search=Matthew+18&version=TPT) (accessed 11 June, 2019).

Chapter 6

Beginnings and Endings

Children do not have the ability to perceive "the big picture." Their lives are still mostly self-centered, and it takes a while under the best of circumstances to learn to share, and to realize that what hurts them also hurts others. Childhood wounding keeps adults self-centered and unable to see "the big picture." The forever loser uses lies, darkness, smokescreens, shadows, camouflage, magnifiers, deceptions, imitations, counterfeits, etc. to keep us from seeing "the big picture."

But the "big picture" is much bigger than we can actually comprehend. That's why we have to become child**like** to trust our loving Father. Remember how vast the heavens are? That's how amazing and great His plans are for us.

Let us gain a heavenly perspective about the appearances of things. We have a promise of something grand and beautiful like an oak tree, but we frown when we are handed an acorn. "That's so small! It tastes bitter! What good is that?" And unless we have the good sense to plant it in the ground, we will never see the promise come to pass—not because the promise wasn't good, but because we despised the process.

Everything worth having is worth waiting for, hoping for and trusting our loving, Almighty Heavenly Father, even when the circumstances don't appear to hold anything good. Although He keeps things hidden sometimes, "**we know** that all things work together for good to them that love God, to them who are the called according to His purpose" (Romans 8:28).

His promise in Jeremiah 29:11 is a strong foundation on which to build our expectations: "For I know the thoughts that I think toward you, saith the LORD, thoughts of peace, and not of evil, to give you a future and a hope."[1] Our trust in Him begins to blossom into revelation as our confidence in His Word, character, and reputation grows.

Our trust in Him provides a deep, inner peace that enables us to serve Him with gladness even when we don't understand.

I remember a time in my young adulthood when I was going through severe mental torment. Thankfully, I have been so healed from the episode that I don't have any recall of what the torment was. What I do remember was that the Holy Spirit in me would bubble up with this heartfelt prayer: "Lord, I don't understand, but I love You and I trust You!" I don't recall how many weeks or months the test went on, but I know that the Lord protected my love and deep trust to counterbalance the overwhelming onslaught of darkness that overshadowed me. I came out victoriously with a deeper trust in God than I had ever had.

Things never seem to end as they begin. That's why we mustn't neglect to say "thank you" to our Father when He provides an acorn. Let's look at a few lessons from life that illustrate this principle.

---

1   Jeremiah 29:11, *JPS Tanakh 1917*. https://biblehub.com/jeremiah/29-11.htm (acessed 13 June 2019).

Day Begins with Night

Scripturally, the day begins with night. In Genesis 1, each day was declared as being the evening and morning. So when we have labored until the sun goes down, at that point the new day begins. That why we are admonished, "Don't let the sun go down on your anger."[2] In other words, if you get upset about something, if you get irritated, exasperated or indignant, deal with it before the end of the day. Let it go. Forgive. Don't take it to bed with you or it may affect your dreams—worse still, it can open you up to demonic torment.

When one keeps the Sabbath, all work ceases when the sun goes down. In Israel, you can feel the rest settling in. The shops close early, the busses stop running, and the streets get quiet. And for a bit more than 24 hours (they like to make it last!) there is a calm. The observant walk to their synagogues for prayer before their festive evening meal, and even many of the non-observant have friends over for dinner.

Learn to see that God designed us to begin our day with rest. When the sun goes down, so should the stresses of the day. Perhaps you are tired, or even exhausted, but realize that it's a new day. It's not the same day as when the sun came up. The sun comes up in the middle of that new 24-hour period, so the day is half over before you have to start working! Get a new mindset from God's perspective! The "big picture" is that darkness precedes light, but light has the last word!

Birth Begins with Pain

"A woman when she is in travail has sorrow, because her hour is come: but as soon as she is delivered of the child, she remembers no more the anguish, for joy that a man is born into the world" (John 16:21). No pregnant

2   Ephesians 4:26

woman looks forward to her labor except to get it over with. She has probably prepared a nursery or at least a bassinet or crib (maybe a box or a drawer if they are very poor). She has been pondering what to name the child and wondering who the child will look like. But she may dread the birthing process! Modern medicine has taken much of the pain out of the process for the faint of heart or those whose childbirth becomes too painful to stand. But women have been doing this since Eve, the "mother of all living," and Jesus' words play out for mother after mother that the joy of the infant is worth the pain of childbirth.

Adulthood Begins with Infancy

Only God can see the end from the beginning. It is impossible for us to see, for instance, what kind of adult a baby will become. Perhaps the child looks like her daddy when she's born, but she looks like her mom in her teen years, then she grows up to look like her maternal grandmother. But all adults start out as babies—eating, sleeping, crying, filling diapers, throwing temper tantrums. All that is expected of babies. But as wonderful as that little life is, it's going to be a long time before they can be trusted with the keys to the car!

A mother who declares over her babe in arms, "This is my son, the doctor," is seeing the end from the beginning. That may or may not be the actual destiny for the child, but declaring greatness over her child can be a great help in developing into his/her God-given destiny.

In the same way, we must trust the Lord and speak His "big picture" promises over our small, and perhaps traumatic beginnings.

Resurrection Begins with Death[3]

Mary and Martha were dismayed that Jesus didn't arrive in time. They had sent word to their dearest Friend,

---

3   John 11

the Miracle Worker, to let Him know that their brother, Lazarus, was sick. Their hearts held hope that he would be healed as soon as Jesus arrived, but their hopes were dashed when Lazarus breathed his last breath. Jesus hadn't made it. This was beyond their comprehension. He had never disappointed them before!

The death of their brother was cause for deep mourning, but the pain in their hearts was compounded by the apparent failure of the One they had come to love and trust. Why hadn't He come? Lazarus' death could have been averted if He had only come! Why, O God? Why?

But Jesus had deliberately delayed His arrival. These were some of His dearest friends and He wanted to show them a greater miracle than they had expected. He wouldn't do that for just anybody, even though He loved everyone. No, these were His host family when He came to Jerusalem. He wanted to do something extraordinary for them to illustrate His gratitude for their love and hospitality. So He busied Himself in another part of the country until it was too late—or so they thought! His intent was to raise the level of faith in His disciples as well as Mary and Martha.

Martha went out to meet Him when He arrived. She chided Him, "If You had been here, Lazarus wouldn't have died." She had faith in Him as the Healer. But she dared to take a step of faith and declared, "But I know that, even now, whatever You ask of God, God will give it to You!" She had faith in His faith.

Jesus replied, "Your brother shall rise again."

Martha shifted into natural understanding. "I know that he will rise again in the resurrection at the last day." She thought it was over. She would have to be content to go on living her life without her brother until she joined him in death.

Then Jesus said something she couldn't comprehend. It was "the big picture" that was as high as the heavens are above the earth. "I AM the Resurrection, and the Life: he that believes in Me, though he were dead, yet shall he live: And whosoever lives and believes in Me shall never die. Do you believe this?"

Martha replied, "Yes, Lord: I believe that You are the Messiah, the Son of God, the One Who is to come into the world."

It was still too mysterious—what was Jesus going to do? Anything? Could she dare to hope for a greater miracle than healing?

She ran to fetch her sister Mary who was too heartbroken to move until Martha whispered to her, "The Master has come and He's calling for you." She jumped up and ran to meet Him with the same words Martha had used, lovingly, agonizingly scolding Him for not coming soon enough to save her brother's life. The people who had come to sit *shiva*⁴ with them followed her, thinking she was going to weep at the tomb.

Jesus was moved by the emotion of all the mourning. He groaned in His Spirit and asked to see where Lazarus' body had been laid. Jesus added His tears to theirs. His compassion was greater than they could comprehend, but He groaned over the senselessness of death. If Adam and Eve hadn't eaten the forbidden fruit, Lazarus wouldn't have even gotten sick. The bondage of sin, iniquity, and transgression had imprisoned mankind and corrupted the earth. He was the physical embodiment of Resurrection Life, and He would soon voluntarily lay it down to pay the ransom for all sin. How He longed for that day to free mankind!

---

4   *Shiva* is the Jewish practice of spending seven days mourning with those who have lost a loved one.

But in this moment, He could only produce the acorn. He could only free Lazarus from death on this day, but the oak tree that would grow from this miracle would be so great that acorns of faith would drop in every nation, among every kindred, people and language! Yes, an acorn would do!

Amid the objections of the sisters that after these four days the body would stink, Jesus ordered the stone to be rolled back from the mouth of the cave. He told them that they would see the glory of God if they would believe, then He prayed, "Father, I thank You that You have heard Me. And I knew that You always hear Me: but because of the people who are standing here I said it, so that they may believe that You have sent Me."

Then He called out, "Lazarus, come forth!" And he did! Jesus ordered that they unwrap him from the grave clothes, and faith was born in the hearts of many.

Even Jesus' own resurrection couldn't come until He first died on the cross. Don't be overwhelmed by death. It's the acorn of the oak of resurrection!

Trust in the Face of Death

I was deeply moved by the testimony of Evelyn Rutledge, who told how many years ago she had a wonderful, happy life as a pastor's wife and mother of two small children. She was perfectly content and they had plans for the rest of their lives. One day they were on their way to spend a family vacation. She heard in her spirit, "It's appointment day for three."[5] Shortly thereafter, a truck went out of control and smashed into their Volkswagon, killing her husband and son. Their toddler daughter died a few hours later in the hospital.

When she came to, she heard the Holy Spirit say to her in her heart, "Evelyn, this is My will. I'm going to

---

5   Hebrews 9:27: "... It is appointed unto men once to die, but after this the judgment."

work it all out." She felt as though she was being wrapped in a blanket of the peace of the Lord. She was able to go through the entire ordeal with a calm serenity that made everyone wonder. She told people, "I know they are with the Lord and I will see them again."

When a hearing was held about the accident, the judge ruled that no one was at fault, but that it was "an act of God," like a tornado or a flood. Her deep trust in the Lord and the words she had heard Him whisper in her spirit gave her a confident victory over grief. He walked with her moment by moment, knowing that she could receive this from the hand of her loving Heavenly Father, in spite of how the circumstances looked. She knew that God had a plan, and her life went on in trust, finding Him at every turn, leading, guiding, rebuilding and restoring.[6]

Even though she couldn't see "the big picture" at the time of the accident, she knew that she could trust that "the big God" she served had a big plan. The acorn of this accident became a totally different oak than she had anticipated. She went on to marry another pastor and bore more children as she lived her life to the glory of God.

Harvest Begins with Weeping

"They that sow in tears shall reap in joy. He that goes forth and weeps, bearing precious seed, shall doubtless come again with rejoicing, bringing his sheaves with him" (Psalm 126:5-6).

The context of these verses has to do with the return of the exiles of Israel from Babylon. Very few who returned after 70 years had actually left Israel. Only those who were young when they were carried away now returned as old men and old women. They had sowed in tears in Babylon, and now they had returned to the Land God

---

6   Evelyn Rutledge: https://www.youtube.com/watch?v=dIzgmSfOXr8 (accessed 14 June 2019). Testimony used by permission.

had promised to Abraham, Isaac, and Jacob and their descendants. For centuries the prophets had enjoined the people to obey the Lord and prosper in His pleasure, and they had warned them that the price of their disobedience would be exile. There were seasons of revival and return to serving the Lord. One generation would put away their idols and thus grant a reprieve—a stay of execution of the promised judgment.

The time came, however, when the cup of iniquity was full. Idolatry, ritual prostitution, and child sacrifice had gone on too long with no repentance. The Land hadn't been given its sabbatical rest every seventh year for seventy cycles, so the exile went on for seventy years to fulfil those years of rest the Land hadn't received. For seventy years the Israelites wept by the rivers of Babylon. They couldn't return to the Promised Land to keep the three annual Feasts of the Lord. Each of those feasts is a celebration of harvest. Passover celebrates the barley harvest. Shavuot (Pentecost) celebrates the wheat harvest, and Sukkot (Tabernacles) celebrates the processing of the grain, grapes into wine, olives into oil, and the ingathering of other produce.

Each year in Babylon they sowed in tears and they longed for the day when they could return to the Land Promised to their forefathers. And when they did, their harvests were full of joy, returning to celebrate the feasts of harvest—festivals of joy! Now the harvest was coming from THEIR Land. Somehow they had survived day-to-day in Babylon, but their tears had given way to elation. The sins of their fathers had been forgiven, and now they could celebrate the way God intended.

Now imagine how the Jewish people have felt for nearly two millennia of exile. Their prayers for all those years included supplications to God to allow them to return to their Land. How many years? How many tears?

The few Jews who remained in the Land through the centuries would go to the Western retaining Wall of the Temple Mount and weep for the restoration. That's why it was known as the "Wailing Wall."

In many nations the Jews weren't even allowed to own land. There wasn't even any possibility sowing of agricultural seed for them. That's why they became providers of services, bankers, jewellers, retailers, etc. So because the blessings of Jacob were upon them, and because their prayers included blessing the Lord and thanking Him for their daily bread and for giving them life, many prospered. God hasn't ever forgotten His covenant with them. His promises have always been for good, even when it looked so bad! Even when they were persecuted, tortured, and killed, God's promises were still there. How much weeping can a people endure? And then came the most horrific of all—the Holocaust, the *Shoah*. The insane schemes of the Nazi regime worked hand-in-glove with satan to try to eliminate God's people before the set time would come for them to be restored to the Land.

The Land had been mourning for them to return. It was desolate, barren, hopeless.

Psalm 102:3-5, 8-9 describes the desperate scene of the Nazi death camps:

> For my days are consumed like smoke, and my bones are burned as a hearth. My heart is smitten, and withered like grass; so that I forget to eat my bread. By reason of the voice of my groaning my bones cleave to my skin.... My enemies reproach me all the day; and they that are mad against me are sworn against me. For I have eaten ashes like bread, and mingled my drink with weeping....

But the promise was nearly within reach. The process had already begun in the mid 1800s when Jews from Eastern Europe followed their hearts back to the Land.

Some 140,000 Holocaust survivors returned to Israel in the years following World War II.

Psalm 102 continues in verses 13-22:

You shalt arise, and have mercy upon Zion: **for the time to favour her, yea, the set time, is come.** For your servants take pleasure in her stones, and favour the dust thereof [archeologists]. So the heathen shall fear the name of the Lord, and all the kings of the earth your glory. **When the Lord shall build up Zion, he shall appear in His glory.** He will regard the prayer of the destitute, and not despise their prayer. This shall be written for the generation to come: and the people which shall be created shall praise the Lord. For he has looked down from the height of His sanctuary; from heaven did the Lord behold the earth; To hear the groaning of the prisoner; to loose those that are appointed to death; To declare the name of the Lord in Zion, and His praise in Jerusalem; When the people are gathered together, and the kingdoms, to serve the Lord.

Satan had tried to destroy God's Chosen People before they could return to their Land. He was trying to prevent the building up of Zion and the appearance of the Lord in His glory. But he's the forever loser, and although the death toll was six million, he could not succeed in stopping the plan for good of the Almighty.

When they returned to the Land, they had to learn how to farm. They sowed in tears, not even knowing how to do it. They moved rocks and labored to restore the soil that had been eroded during centuries of neglect. But their joy was full when the earth began to yield her strength once again to the people she had been waiting for. The harvest that began with tears came in with the joy of God's promises fulfilled.

Fine Gold Begins with Fire

"...You, who are kept by the power of God through faith unto salvation ready to be revealed in the last time. Wherein you greatly rejoice, though now for a season, if need be, you are in heaviness through manifold temptations: That the trial of your faith, being much more precious than of gold that perishes, though it be tried with fire, might be found unto praise and honour and glory at the appearing of Jesus Christ" (1 Peter 1:4-7).

Gold appears in nature as an alloy with other minerals. Its value is determined by its purity. Ten karat gold is gold. It has value as gold. But if you want to increase its value, you put it through the fire. The melting point of gold is 1,948°F (1,064°C). That's mighty hot! But if you want to purify it, gold has to endure that terrible ordeal of heat. It can become 18 karat gold. More fire produces fine gold—24 karat gold.

That should give us some perspective of what God might be up to when He allows trials in our lives. He is refining us for the day of His coming! We don't know what kind of blessings can come out of tragedies or traumas. But we can trust that the One Who is coming, the Great Refiner, knows how much we can bear, and He promises to be with us throughout the whole process to His glorious expected end.

"But He knows the way that I take: when He has tried me, I shall come forth as gold" (Job 23:10).

"And I will bring the third part through the fire, and will refine them as silver is refined, and will try them as gold is tried: they shall call on My name, and I will hear them: I will say, It is my people: and they shall say, The LORD is my God" (Zechariah 13:9). "Yea, though I walk through the valley of the shadow of death, I will fear no evil: for you are with me" (Psalm 23:4).

Chapter 7
Overcomers

"These things I have spoken unto you, that in me you might have peace. In the world you shall have tribulation: but be of good cheer; I have overcome the world" (John 16:33).

Jesus is our model, our example, of what it looks like to overcome. When He took the keys of Hell and Death, He paraded the defeated adversary through the heavenlies as the Almighty Conqueror.[1] The word in Greek for "overcome" is "Strong's G3528, *nikáō*, [pronounced] nik-ah'-o; from G3529; to subdue (literally or figuratively):— conquer, overcome, prevail, get the victory."

The Outline of Biblical Usage renders this word:

I. to conquer

    A. to carry off the victory, come off victorious

        i. of Christ, victorious over all His foes

        ii. of Christians, that hold fast their faith even unto death against the power of their foes, and temptations and persecutions

---

1   Colossians 2:15

iii. when one is arraigned or goes to law, to win the case, maintain one's cause[2]

When we have Jesus in our life, the Overcomer lives inside of us, and He gives us the grace, strength, and power to overcome any obstacle. He also told His disciples a key that we must embrace: "I am the vine, you are the branches: He that abides in me, and I in Him, the same brings forth much fruit: for **without me you can do nothing**" (John 15:5).

The Apostle Paul gave these orders through the inspiration of the Holy Spirit: "Be not overcome of evil, but overcome evil with good" (Romans 12:21). That's a command! Overcome evil with good! Every evil that has taken place in our lives can be transformed into good, that is, a *rich wound* that will bring glory to God and great fruit in our lives and great rewards in eternity.

Revelation 12:10-11 expresses that the accuser of the brethren (the forever loser) is overcome by the Blood of the Lamb and the word of our testimony (and we don't love our lives unto death). We have the weapons (Jesus' Blood and our words) and we have the Mighty Conqueror living inside us.[3] We can do this!

The Apostle John explains that whoever is born of God overcomes the world. It's just what we do. It's Christian Life 101. And it's our faith that does the overcoming—our very believing, trusting that Jesus is the Son of God,[4] that He is the Truth. We know that Truth always overcomes lies and deceit. When we embrace eternal Truth, the Light vanquishes the darkness and we are set free!

---

2   *Nikao, Blue Letter Bible.* https://www.blueletterbible.org/lang/lexicon/lexicon. cfm?Strongs=G3528&t=KJV (accessed 12 June 2019).

3   1 John 4:4

4   Ibid. 5:4-5

In the Book of Revelation, there are many promises to overcomers:

- To him that overcomes will I give to eat of the tree of life, which is in the midst of the paradise of God.

- He that overcomes shall not be hurt of the second death.

- To him that overcomes will I give to eat of the hidden manna, and will give him a white stone, and in the stone a new name written, which no man knows saving he that receives it.

- And he that overcomes, and keeps My works unto the end, to him will I give power over the nations.

- He that overcomes, the same shall be clothed in white raiment; and I will not blot out his name out of the book of life, but I will confess his name before My Father, and before His angels.

- Him that overcomes will I make a pillar in the temple of My God, and he shall go no more out: and I will write upon him the name of My God, and the name of the city of My God, which is new Jerusalem, which comes down out of heaven from My God: and I will write upon him My new name....

- To him that overcomes will I grant to sit with me in My throne, even as I also overcame, and am set down with My Father in His throne.[5]

And at the end of the book comes the greatest promise: He that overcomes shall inherit all things; and I will be his God, and he shall be My son.[6]

---

5   Revelation 2: 7, 11, 17, 26, 3:5, 12, 21

6   Ibid. 21:7

They Did It! Testimonies of Overcomers

Forgiveness and Salvation for Uncle

Ann B. Shares this testimony:

At the age of 17, my mother's brother committed armed robbery (among other things) and was sent to the penitentiary for twenty years. During this time, I, as a little girl, went with my grandmother and his wife, and other family members to visit him. While incarcerated he was in the post for all sort of things like reading for the blind and making different kind of plaques and things.

When he was released I guess I kind of looked up to him for some reason that I can't explain. One night when I was 13 years old, he came to my grandmother's house and asked if I wanted to go and stay the night with one of his girlfriends who was young and we would smoke weed together and just have fun. I wanted to go and my grandmother didn't know I was going to smoke weed, so she didn't mind me going.

When we left, he drove me to a back street and parked on a lot. I immediately knew something was wrong, but what was I going to do? He then took out two needles and he shot me up with cocaine and heroin, then he injected himself and told me that if I told anyone he would tell that I wanted it. Prior to this one time I heard my mother and her sister and friends talking about this kind of thing happening to someone they knew being molested by a relative. My mother said if it was to happen to one of her children that she would kill the person who did it. If you knew my mother, you would know that she meant it. So with that and him saying that he would tell people that I wanted it, I never told.

From then on, I always said if he was to die I would spit in his face. That's how I thought about him with no regrets. Twenty years later at age 33, I received salvation. My uncle got sick about a year and a half into my born again experience with Christ, and he was put on life support. God began to deal with me and put on my heart that I had to witness to him. I know that it was God and not me. So my friend and I went to see him. I had her to take his girlfriend out of the room. I called his name and I could see the fear on his face; he knew it was me. Then I told him that I forgave him for all of the things that he had ever done to me, and that Jesus saved me and wanted to forgive him as well. I told him that if he would repent and ask the LORD to come into his heart and believe that He died for his sins and was raised at the right hand of God, that he could receive forgiveness and salvation. Then I left.

About two days later I had a dream that this light was shining on this certain spot that was dark and it was snowing in this area. When I woke up, I knew that he had died and he had received salvation. My phone rang and I was told that he was dead. Isaiah 1:18 gave sense to the dream, "Come now, and let us reason together, saith the Lord: though your sins be as scarlet, they shall be as white as snow; though they be red like crimson, they shall be as wool."

This is my testimony that when God says that it is not His will that any man shall perish, but that all come into the knowledge of God, He means it, when He says that He has taken our sins upon

Himself, He has. His ways are truly not ours and His love is unfathomable. My uncle was able to receive Jesus on his death bed and I was able to forgive. God used me out of all people to witness to him. I truly know the tender mercies of God. Amen.

Raped! God's Grace is Sufficient

Sister M. shares:

I was robbed and raped by two men in the early morning hours of June 1, 1991. As soon as the men left, I picked up my Bible and started reading out loud the first five Psalms (I read five per day). The next thing I recall was all this love being poured into my heart and like a whooshing sound. I was lifted up into heavenly places. Then out of my spirit came the song "My Glory and the Lifter of My Head." I sang this song over and over for many days.

The same afternoon of the incident, the Lord said for me to pray for the two men. I had no anger, resentment towards them! I told the Lord, "First I'll forgive them" and then I prayed. I have no idea how I prayed—probably in tongues. Days later the Lord said, "This is how I want you to pray for these two men: as Jesus said, 'Father, forgive them for they know not what they do,' and as Stephen prayed, 'Father, lay not this sin to their charge.'"

Every day I prayed for these two men after first meditating on I Corinthians 13:4-8a (AMP) especially verse 5 which says, "I'll take no account of the evil done to me not to a suffered wrong."

From the beginning, the Lord said as I would read His Word, the Word (Jesus) would heal me.

It was very hard to come back home and be by myself after spending some weeks with family members. From the first day I kept prophesying that I would have to go through this. Twice I had to return to my family to get some sleep.

During this time, I meditated on fear scriptures (man and God's) and on peace and healing.

I was also praying for the police and special investigators for my case, that God would give them success; this was done in love.

I praise God for the gift of tongues to help me pray during the night hours against the fear and terror.

In September, the Lord spoke to me through the book of Jonah. I was no longer to pray that the police would capture these men. That night was the first night I slept in over three months.

I continued to pray for the two men and their salvation. On Sunday, October 6th, the Lord said I was to no longer call them my enemies, but my brothers. The burden was lifted. I believe with all my heart that these two men are now saved. And isn't this what it's all about, to get people saved? Glory to God! I can't believe it only took four months to get the victory! To God be the glory, the lifter of my head!

Three weeks ago, the Holy Spirit led me to praise the Lord for allowing me to go through this experience. All for His eternal purposes.

During this time (June-October) I felt the prayers of the saints and I knew I wasn't alone in this. Others were being my Aarons and Hurs. I want to thank you and all End-Time Handmaidens and Servants who prayed for me. God is so good.

The Anointing Breaks the Yoke

M.T. writes:

I want to tell you how God used Gwen Shaw's book, *Day by Day,* to minister to a close relative of mine.

Some time ago, this young woman (wife of a pastor) was coming out of an office about 7:00 p.m. when two men grabbed her and put her into a van. They beat, raped and tortured her for four hours and left her for dead. She doesn't know who found her and got her to the hospital. She was in a mental institution for two months.

By many, many prayers, God restored her enough so she could go home. She was on a lot of medicine (I mean a lot!) to be able to function. She had depression, panic attacks, nightmares, etc. She had to have someone with her all the time. In these years God has been healing and restoring.

Then in March, she had a malignant tumor removed and six weeks of radiation therapy.

She told me that on June 17 she was walking through the house praying and telling the Lord she couldn't go on in the physical condition she was in. She said clearly the Lord said, "Go read the devotion in *Day by Day*" (June 17). She said she read it every day but usually at night before bedtime. She said it was like an audible voice said the scripture reference: "Psalm 71:20, 21." God did deliver her at that very time. She is beaming! The people of the church could tell the difference in her. She is off all medicine but one hormone pill. Praise God! She is taking some business courses in college. She hadn't been able to remember until June 17. In fact, the doctor had told her husband that she'd be in a mental institution to stay. I wouldn't accept that report! God has the final word! Praise God!

Overcome by Laughter

Emily Osterloh did a lot of biblical counselling. She wrote about this incident in her book, *Vignettes of God's Love, Small Stories of God's Ministry to People in Crisis.*[7]

What a joy it is to know that God laughs (Psalm 2:4). When counseling at a woman's retreat I shared in the joy as the Lord restored laughter to a woman who had lost her laughter many years before because of anger, bitterness, and the load of responsibility she had taken upon herself.

She came into our counseling room wobbling from the oxygen container she dragged with her, emphysema from smoking she told us. Lips pressed together, a frown on her face, she was the picture of anger and frustration. She talked, then as the Lord began to take her back to the roots she became very quiet. Her eyes became wet. I expected tears but she suddenly broke into laughter. She laughed and laughed, then stopped in amazement and gasped, "He has given me back my laughter."

She had been raped at thirteen, repeatedly been told she was stupid, felt unworthy and had taken on responsibilities for her adult children that were no longer hers. As the Lord ministered to her she murmured, "I'm beautiful and precious. I don't need to feel bad. I'm not bad. I'm OK. I can laugh again. I haven't laughed in years and years. Now all of that seems funny."

---

7 Emily Osterloh. *Vignettes of God's Love, Small Stories of God's Ministry to People in Crisis* (Jasper: Engeltal Press, 2004).

She continued to laugh. Her head became erect. We laughed with her. As she thanked the Lord for what He had done she broke into smiles and her face became beautiful. Now weeks later when thinking of her I begin to laugh... and get my daily dose of heavenly medicine. Proverbs 17:22 "A merry heart does good like a medicine."

"He Could Trust You with the Scars"

"Eight months into his tour of duty in Vietnam, Dave Roever was burned beyond recognition when a phosphorous grenade he was poised to throw exploded in his hand. The ordeal left him hospitalized for fourteen months, where he underwent numerous major surgeries. His survival and life are miraculous."[8]

In his blog on February 2, 2017, he wrote this:

For years, I have shared the story of Jan Crouch saying to me, while live on the set of the *Praise the Lord* program, "Dave, God didn't put those scars on your face. But He didn't stop it because He knew He could trust you with the scars." I've shared the impact that statement made in my life and how the Lord used it to set me free from the demon of suicide.

Sunday night, I was honored to speak to a group of churches that gathered for a wonderful night of worship. The minister who introduced me is the leader of the pastors of those churches, and many more in North Texas, but most importantly, he is my friend. He made another statement that will forever change how I view the occurrence in my life on July 26, 1969.

He said, "It must have been a hard day in heaven when God saw what was happening to Dave,

---

8   http://roeverfoundation.org/meet_dave_roever.php (accessed 24 June 2019).

knowing He could stop it. Instead, He allowed it, also knowing Dave could handle the devastation and use it for the glory of God." Wow! My heart was torn between brokenness and joy, at the sound of his words.

"A hard day in heaven…"

I realize I am not the only person on this planet who has been hurt, devastated, ripped to pieces, put back together again and lived to tell about it. Many of you reading this email have also been hurt, deeply. I share these statements with you in an attempt to encourage you, as I have been encouraged.

What has happened in your life that made it a "hard day in heaven" for God to allow His child to go through the fire? What has happened to you that God would say, "I can trust you with this trial"?

It's your choice to view your circumstances in the appropriate way. Choose today to understand that God can use ALL things for His glory, no matter how horrible it may seem today. Remember that God is not in heaven rejoicing at your tragedy. He is a loving God who allows things to happen so that His glory is revealed.

Love, Dave

"See, I have refined you, though not as silver; I have tested you in the furnace of affliction" (Isaiah 48:10). [9]

The Rewards Are Out of This World!

Dr. David Yonggi Cho's associate pastor died of heart attack, but was sent back by the Lord. His name is Pastor

Sang Ho Kim. When he arrived in Heaven, he asked the angel about his wife who had passed away five days earlier. He was told, "as a matter of fact, you are here at her request." When he went to her mansion, he saw her coming out, and noticed a beautiful diamond shining from the back of her head.

When they had been young, one Sunday they went to church instead of working in the rice paddy. His father was so angry that he picked up a rock and threw it at her, hitting the back of her head. She had a scar there all of her life. In Heaven, however, that scar was shining like a diamond. The pastor was told that when you receive persecution, all of those things are going to be rewarded.[10] This is truly a *rich wound*!

Rejoicing for Suffering

In the book of the Acts of the Apostles, the Holy Spirit was being poured out in a powerful way and tremendous signs and miracles were happening. The High Priest (who wasn't really the legitimate one, but one who received a favour from Rome to get the appointment to that office) and his cohorts were overwhelmed with jealous indignation, and had the apostles arrested. During the night, an angel rescued them from the prison and gave them instructions to go and preach openly in the temple.

When the council came together the next day, they sent for the prisoners. The messengers returned without them. They had found the cell closed, secure, and guarded, but it was empty. Just then, informants came rushing in with the news that the men who had been imprisoned were teaching in the temple!

The captain of the temple guard was sent to arrest them peaceably, lest a riot ensue. The High Priest

---

10   Dr. David Yonggi Cho. https://www.youtube.com/watch?v=tbZNp141Vno (accessed 12 June 2019).

questioned them about their disobedience to the orders they had given them not to teach in the name of Jesus.

Peter replied, "We must listen to and obey God more than pleasing religious leaders. You had Jesus arrested and killed by crucifixion, but the God of our forefathers has raised Him up. He's the one God has exalted and seated at His right hand as our Savior and Champion. He is the provider of grace as the Redeemer of Israel. We are witnesses of these things, and so is the Holy Spirit, whom God freely gives to all who believe in Him."[11]

This infuriated the High Priest who was ready to kill them! Then Gamliel (also known as Gamaliel, the grandson of Hillel), a man known for his great wisdom, exhorted the Sanhedrin to exercise caution in deciding what to do with these men. He reasoned that the devotees of other rabble-rousers dispersed when the leaders died. Then he warned them that if this controversial activity was from man it would wane to nothing, but if it were of God, they should be very careful, lest they be fighting against God! (And here we are nearly 2,000 years later!)

So the council decided to have them beaten and released. "The apostles left there **rejoicing, thrilled that God had considered them worthy to suffer disgrace for the name of Jesus.**"[12]

These were true overcomers who were willing to give up their lives for the Truth! And the Truth is still marching on!

---

11 Acts 5:29-32

12 Ibid. 5:41

Chapter 8

Counted Worthy to Suffer

"Take, my brethren, the prophets, who have spoken in the name of the Lord, for an example of suffering affliction, and of patience. Behold, we count them happy [blessed] which endure. You have heard of the patience of Job, and have seen the end of the Lord; that the Lord is very pitying, and of tender mercy [compassion]" (James 5:10-11).

Whenever the subject of suffering is being discussed, the name that nearly always comes up is Job.

Using adjectives chosen by various Bible translators, Job is described as:

- blameless and upright; he feared God and shunned evil. (NIV)

- blameless—a man of complete integrity. He feared God and stayed away from evil. (NLT)

- a man of perfect integrity, who feared God and turned away from evil. (HCSB)

- whole-hearted and upright, and one that feared God, and shunned evil. (JPS Tanakh 1917)

81

- true, blameless, righteous, and godly, abstaining from everything evil. (Brenton Septuagint Translation, 1884)
- simple and upright, and fearing God, and avoiding evil. (Douay-Rheims)
- perfect and upright—both fearing God, and turning aside from evil. (YLT)[1]

He had seven sons and three daughters. He was extremely wealthy with huge flocks of seven thousand sheep, three thousand camels, five hundred yoke of oxen, five hundred donkeys, and many servants. He was the wealthiest man in the region.

When his grown children would get together for a feast, Job stood up before the Lord as the High Priest of his household to make intercession for them in case they had sinned or their hearts had been turned away from God. He made sacrifices to cover their sins before God, offering the blood of animals to atone them, much like parents today plead the blood of Jesus over their children, even when they are grown. He was extending his fatherly cloak of integrity over them as the patriarch of his household. Job's worship went up and the blessings came down.

The Setup

One day when the Almighty was holding court, the adversary (accuser) came along with the sons of God. When our Father, the Judge of all the earth, questioned his activities, he replied that he had been roaming around the earth in every direction (he's not omni-present!).

Then God asks a strange question: "Have you considered My servant Job? For there is no one on earth like him, a man who is blameless and upright, who fears God and shuns evil."

---

1   Job 1:1 https://biblehub.com/job/1-1.htm (accessed 15 June 2019).

Our Father knew Job's heart and had noted all of his characteristics. God declared Job to be:

- Blameless
- Upright
- Reverent toward God
- One who turns away from evil.

God, Who IS truth and can only speak truth, has nothing at all negative to say about Job. He finds no fault in him. He's pleased with him. When God says you are good, you are good!

Well, of course satan had considered Job. He had been studying how he could trip him up and get a legal opportunity to attack him—but he hadn't found any way to get through God's hedge of protection. God's pleasure with Job's uprightness had surrounded Job like a force field. The forever loser sneered, "Why shouldn't Job reverence You? You have Your hedge of protection around him, his household, and all he owns! You bless everything he does, and his livestock just keep multiplying and increasing his wealth." He steamed with rage as he spat out the accusation: "But if You touch his stuff, just You watch—he'll curse You to Your face!"

Inwardly, the Lord chuckled. Satan had taken His bait. He knew Job's heart, that he loved and acknowledged Him for everything. Job did not consider that his life consisted of his wealth. And God loves to set up the forever loser to lose again and again. His relationship with Job was so good that He wanted to bless Job with a special visitation. Yes, Job had been so faithful! He was so trustworthy!

Before He had said, "Let there be light," God looked ahead and saw Job. He saw his beginning and his ending, with everything in between. He knew that Job could be trusted to pass this test. Our Father wanted to give Job a special encounter—a face-to-face encounter with Him in the whirlwind of His Presence.

"Look, I give you permission to touch all that he has, only you can't touch him."

Gleefully, the adversary left to devise the plans to undo all of Job's substance and wipe out his family. He would make it a big production—overwhelming! Certainly! How malevolently delightful to make a multi-pronged attack that would bring him to utter despair and make him lose his heart toward God!

He would even torment Job with threatenings of what he was about to do. He sent his imps to whisper to Job's mind that the marauding Sabeans were nearby. "They stole your neighbor's cattle and donkeys, killing his herdsmen—yours are next!"

Job's dreams would be laced with imaginations of fire falling from heaven and consuming his sheep and shepherds.

The next night he dreamed that the Chaldeans stole his camels and killed his servants who kept them.

Then as he offered sacrifices for his sons and daughters, a macabre motion picture played out on the screen of his imagination: a terrible driving wind took down the corners of his eldest son's house while he and his siblings enjoyed their festive meal. They were all killed, including the servants.

Poor Job! The mental torment plagued him. He couldn't understand where all this was coming from.

Then the day came to execute the plan. BAM! BAM! BAM! BAM! The scenes played out with only one servant surviving to tell each tale.

- Oxen and donkeys STOLEN!
- Sheep CONSUMED by fire!

- Camels CARRIED AWAY!
- Children KILLED!

According to the custom of his culture, Job tore his robe, shaved his head, and lowered himself to sit *shiva*. This was delightful to the adversary! Yes! Get him overwhelmed with mourning!

But wait! What's he doing now? No! NO! NOOOO!

And Job worshipped! He prostrated himself before the Lord and with childlike faith acknowledged His sovereignty. "I came into this world naked and I'll leave the same way. Yehovah gave and Yehovah has taken away. Blessed be the name of Yehovah."

And God Smiled

So on another day God was holding court for the sons of God and the forever loser came with them to present his case.

The Judge said, "Where have you been?"

"Roaming in every direction on the earth," he hissed with contempt.

"Soooo—what do you think about My servant Job now? There's nobody like him in the earth, is there? He is blameless and upright, he reveres Me and shuns evil. He has maintained his integrity even though you incited Me to destroy him WITHOUT CAUSE!"

"Yeah, but he's still only worshipping you because you saved his hide. Reach out Your hand and touch his flesh and bones and he'll renounce You to Your face!"

"Look, I put him in your hand, only you can't take his life!"

So the forever loser masterminded his best scheme to torment Job with pain and rejection. "That's it! BOILS! From head to toe! He'll be in total agony from the pain, and he'll be so ugly and smell so putrid that no one will be able to stand to be around him!'"

And so it was that Job was afflicted with agonizing suffering in his body. He sat in the ashes and scraped his itching skin with a broken piece of pottery. His grief was unbearable.

Then the accuser came from another angle. Job's wife had patiently endured with him the loss of their children and all of their belongings—she couldn't bear to see him suffer like this. "Give it up, Job! This is too much! I don't get how God could allow all this suffering. It's not like Him. Just renounce Him so you can die and end this anguish and misery!"

But Job, with integrity to the core, replied, "You've got to be kidding, my dear! Don't talk like those silly women who can't reason! Shall we accept only good from God's hand? Shall we only trust Him when we see good circumstances? Shall we not also receive evil with trust in Him?" IN ALL THIS JOB DIDN'T SIN WITH HIS LIPS.

Three Friends

Three friends of Job came to sit *shiva* with him. They could see how great his grief was and the whole seven days they sat with him in silence.

Then Job began by cursing the night he was conceived. He was suffering so much that he was wishing he had never been born. He questioned why he didn't die at birth so none of this would have happened.

"The threats of evil that filled my mind with fear have come to pass!"

Don't think that Job's fear was an open door to satan. God Himself said that the accuser had incited Him against Job WITHOUT CAUSE! Job's integrity was intact, even though he didn't understand what was happening and he had been tormented with fear from the devil's threatenings.

Then a new torment began. Job's three friends spent chapters surmising and accusing Job of having done something to cause all this trouble. But Job was innocent! The forever loser had a plan to provoke Job to give up his faith in God. He was certain that Job had an evil, self-seeking place somewhere deep down. He was determined to find that button and push it.

In all the words back and forth, complaining, accusing, defending, incredulity—Job suffered yet more. He didn't understand. But through it all, Job made some tremendous statements of faith that showed his unwavering trust in God, no matter how the circumstances appeared.

"For I know that my redeemer lives, and that He shall stand at the latter day upon the earth: And though after my skin worms destroy this body, yet in my flesh shall I see God" (Job 19:25-26).

"Yet He knows the way I have taken; when He has tested me, I will emerge as pure gold" (Job 23:10 HCSB).

Enough is Enough!

Then the Almighty stepped in. He roared on the scene in a whirlwind and spoke, chiding Job for his misunderstanding of His greatness. In chapters 38-41 He speaks of mysteries that are beyond Job's comprehension and challenges him with questions about "Where were you when I..." He was demonstrating to Job and his friends that He was greater than all their musings about Him. His ways are so much higher than man's!

In the middle of God's monologue, Job humbled himself and stated that he would cover his mouth and not answer.[2] He had clearly misunderstood God and repented

2   Job 40:3-5

87

of questioning His wisdom. He had heard the accuser (the forever loser) in his mind, in his dreams, through his wife, through his friends. The onslaught had been terrible.

Then God went on declaring His ways, and Job finally found words for the revelation of God's motives in all this suffering: "I have heard of You by the hearing of the ear: **but now my eye sees You**" (Job 42:5).

Job's heart had been changed. God's purpose had been accomplished! It was all about increasing Job's awareness of His greatness and glory. Now it was time for the trial to end.

God reprimanded Job's three friends and gave them instructions to offer sacrifices and have Job pray for them.

One of the greatest things we can do when we are going through a test that we don't understand is to intercede for the people that are involved in the misunderstanding— even before they repent!

The glorification process from the Lord started for Job when he first he lost all his livestock and children. Job worshipped, so the glory went up again, completing the circuit. Satan gets a second opportunity and afflicts Job with infirmity and creepy friends. When Job at the end prays for his friends, he glorifies God again God downloads a double portion back down on Job. That is glorification!

In the beginning, Job was already the weightiest of all the men of the East—he was the most prosperous in the known world at the time. The horrific process he went through doubled his glory. The number of his children was also doubled because the first set were still existing on the other side of the grave. And in spite of all the ugliness that Job endured, his second set of daughters were the most beautiful women in the land. Job lived another 140 years and saw four generations of his offspring.

The Bible doesn't specify how long Job's ordeal of undeserved suffering lasted, but it was probably months. Even if it had been two years, in hindsight, Job surely

Chapter 9

The Blessed Rejoice

"**Blessed** are they which are **persecuted** for righteousness' sake: for theirs is the Kingdom of Heaven. **Blessed** are you, when men shall **revile** you, and **persecute** you, and shall **say all manner of evil against you falsely, for My** sake. **Rejoice**, and **be exceeding glad**: for great is your reward in Heaven: for so persecuted they the prophets which were before you" (Matthew 5:10-12).

Jesus promised that persecution and tribulation would come.[1] It began with His death as a sacrifice and has continued ever since. Tragically, the number of martyrdoms for our Messiah annually continues to rise. The twentieth century had more deaths from persecution than all the previous nineteen centuries combined.[2]

Every month, on average:

- 345 Christians are killed for faith-related reasons
- 105 Churches and Christian buildings are burned or attacked

---

1   Matthew 10:23, Matthew 24:9, Luke 21:17

2   https://www.christianity.com/church/church-history/centuries/20th-century-11631980.html (accessed 16 June 2019).

- 219 Christians are detained without trial, arrested, sentenced and imprisoned[3]

Many of those who are persecuted stand on the scripture that opens this chapter. They believe it is an honour to be imprisoned for their faith, and martyrdom has great reward, according to Revelation 2:10: "Fear none of those things which you shalt suffer: behold, the devil shall cast some of you into prison, that you may be tried; and you shall have tribulation ten days: be you faithful unto death, and I will give you a crown of life."

When I was first exposed to the ministry of our founder, Gwen Shaw, and her co-worker, Sigi, I attended the church service because my sister had invited me to "come hear these women that smuggle Bibles behind the Iron Curtain." I was intrigued. When I heard Sigi, who had been raised in Communist East Berlin, all I could do was cry—I had no idea why. The next time they came to town, I was on the edge of my seat with Sister Gwen's stories of the persecuted brethren in Eastern Europe. She showed pictures of the people they had met.

One pastor and his wife had several children. Some of the younger ones had had their eardrums deliberately pierced at birth by the Communist doctor so that they would never hear the Gospel.

Another photo was of the body of a pastor in a casket. He had been beaten and tortured to death. The places where his flesh had been torn were crudely sewn together.

She told of delivering Bibles by the leading of the Holy Spirit. "Turn left here. Park over there under that tree. Walk five blocks. Go into that building and climb three flights of stairs. Knock on the door of apartment 14. Whisper, 'Hallelujah!'"

---

3   https://www.opendoorsusa.org/christian-persecution/ (accessed 16 June 2019).

The stories went on and on, and my heart was captured for our beloved brethren. I longed to minister to them in their bonds. My prayers were motivated by Hebrews 13:3, "Remember them that are in bonds, as bound with them; and them which suffer adversity, as being yourselves also in the body."

I wanted to smuggle Bibles behind the Iron Curtain, but never had the opportunity before it came down. When I finally got to Russia, we were handing out Bibles freely in the schools and passing out tracts on the streets in the Presence of police! What an amazing change had taken place after seventy years of the bondage of godlessness.

By this time China had opened and we learned more about the horrific persecution there. One testimony stands out above the rest.

In the Garden

An evangelist we met told how he had been arrested multiple times and served his sentences in various prison camps. In the final one before we met him, he was treated viciously, being beaten if he sang to the Lord even softly. He wasn't permitted to repeat any scriptures aloud, nor could he pray in any way that could be recognized. He was watched like a hawk and the slightest infraction brought on cruelty.

Finally, his persecutors decided that they would task him with the ultimate degradation: he would spend his workday shoveling out the cesspool for fertilizer! The stench was beyond awful and he had to wade waist deep in that muck! Disease was rampant in the camp of 60,000 prisoners, so no one wanted to be around the place.

He was absolutely delighted every day when he was lowered into the cesspool, for here he could pray at the top of his lungs, shout scriptures he had memorized, and sing his praises to the Lord. His favorite hymn was "I Come to the Garden Alone," and he would sing it with gusto, calling the cesspool his "garden." Here he could be alone with the Lord with no one to bother him. When he was finished for the day, no one would come near him because he smelled so badly! [4]

His testimony has been an inspiration to me. He truly exemplifies Jesus' admonition that when persecuted we are to "rejoice and be exceeding glad"!

The Apostles

"If we are joined with Him in His sufferings, then we will reign together with Him in His triumph" (2 Timothy 2:12 TPT).

Paul wrote those words to Timothy near the end of his life. As a Roman citizen, he was martyred by beheading around 66 AD.

Probably the same year in the same city, **Peter** laid down his life by being crucified upside down. He didn't feel worthy to die the same way Jesus had, so he requested to hang inverted.

As recorded in Acts 12:2, Herod had **James, the brother of John** and son of Zebedee, killed with the sword about 44 AD.

According to tradition, **Andrew** was crucified in Greece after having brought the Gospel to Russia, which was then known as the "land of the man eaters." He also preached in "Asia," which is modern-day Turkey.

I have been to the place in India where **Thomas** was pierced through by four soldiers' spears. He had preached the Gospel there and founded the church which still upholds the name of Jesus in spite of persecution.

Philip ministered in the North African city of Carthage, then went on to Asia Minor. The wife of the

---

4   https://www.scionofzion.com/cesspool.htm (accessed 16 June 2019).

Roman Proconsul was converted under his preaching and her husband was not pleased. He had Philip arrested and put to death in a cruel way.

Matthew, also known as Levi, was the tax/toll collector who followed Jesus and wrote the first Gospel account. Reports vary about how his life ended, but it is known that he ministered in Persia and Ethiopia where some say he was stabbed to death.

Tradition shows **Bartholomew** as a very active missionary to the nations. He accompanied Thomas to India, travelled to Armenia, Ethiopia, and Southern Arabia. Although accounts disagree as to how he was martyred, it is clear that he gave his life for the Lord.

Josephus, the Jewish historian relates that **James, the son of Alpheus**, was stoned and then clubbed to death following his ministry in Syria.

The story is told that **Simon the Zealot** ministered in Persia where he was killed for refusing to worship their sun god.

Judas, who betrayed Jesus, was replaced by **Matthais**, according to Acts 1:15-26. According to tradition, he went to Syria with Andrew, and was put to death by burning.

It is said of **John** that he was the only one of the disciples who died a natural death from old age. Other traditions say that he never died, probably concluding that from Jesus' statement to Peter, "If I will that he tarry till I come, what is that to you? You follow Me" (John 21:22-23). "During Domitian's persecution in the middle 90s, he was exiled to the island of Patmos. There he is credited with writing the last book of the New Testament—the Revelation. An early Latin tradition has him escaping unhurt after being cast into boiling oil at Rome."[5]

---

5   https://www.christianity.com/church/church-history/timeline/1-300/whatever-happened-to-the-twelve-apostles-11629558.html (accessed 16 June 2019). And http://

The Theban Legion

Under Maximian, who was an Emperor of the Roman Commonwealth (Empire) with Diocletian as his colleague, an uprising of the Gauls known as "Bagaude" forced Maximian to march against them with an army of which one unit was the Theban Legion composed of 6,600 men, [in the spring of 285 AD] in . This unit had been recruited from upper Egypt and consisted entirely of Christians. They were good men and soldiers who, even under arms, did not forget to render to God the things of God, and to Caesar the things of Caesar.

After the revolt was quelled, the Emperor Maximian issued an order that the whole army should join in offering sacrifices to the Roman gods for the success of their mission. The order included killing Christians (probably as a sacrifice to the Roman gods). Only the Theban Legion dared to refuse to comply with the orders. The legion withdrew itself, encamped near Aguanum and refused to take part in these rites.

Maximian was then resting in a near-by place called Octudurum. When the news of their refusal came to him, he repeatedly commanded them to obey his rules and orders, and upon their constant and unanimous refusal, he ordered that the legion should be "decimated." Accordingly, every tenth man was put to death. A second decimation was ordered unless the men obeyed the order given, but there was a great shout through the legion camp: they all declared that they would never allow themselves to carry out such a sacrilegious order. They always had a horror of idolatry; they had been brought up as Christians and were instructed in the One Eternal God and were ready to suffer extreme penalties rather than do anything contrary to their religion.

When Maximian heard this news, he got angrier than ever. Like a savage beast, he ordered the second decimation to be carried out, intending that the remainder should be compelled to do what they hitherto refused. Yet they still maintained their resolve. After the second decimation, Maximian warned the remainder of the Theban Legion that it was of no use for them to trust in their number, for if they persisted in their disobedience, not a man among them would be able to escape death.

The greatest mainstay of their faith in this crisis was undoubtedly their captain, Maurice, with his lieutenants Candid, the first commanding officer, and Exuperius the Compidoctor.[6] He fired the hearts of the soldiers with fervor by his encouragement. Maurice, calling attention to the example of their faithful fellow soldiers, already martyrs, persuaded them all to be ready to die in their turn for the sake of their baptismal vow (the promise one makes at his baptismal to renounce satan and his abominable service and to worship only God). He reminded them of their comrades who had gone to Heaven before them. At his words, a glorious eagerness for martyrdom burned in the hearts of those most blessed men.

Fired thus by the lead of their officers, the Theban Legion sent to Maximian (who was still enraged) a reply as loyal as it is brave:

"Emperor, we are your soldiers but also the soldiers of the true God. We owe you military service and obedience, but we cannot renounce Him who is our Creator and Master, and also yours even though you reject Him. In all things which are not against His law, we most willingly obey you, as we have done hitherto. We readily oppose your enemies whoever they are, but we cannot stain our hands with the blood of innocent people (Christians). We have taken an oath to God before we took one to you, you cannot place any confidence in our second oath if we violate the other (the first). You commanded us to execute Christians, behold we are such. We confess God the Father, the Creator of all things, and His Son Jesus Christ, our God. We have seen our comrades slain with the sword, we do not weep for them but rather rejoice at their honour. Neither this, nor any other provocation have tempted us to revolt. Behold, we have arms in our hands, but we do not resist, because we would rather die innocent than live by any sin."

When Maximian heard this, he realized that these men were obstinately determined to remain in their Christian faith, and he despaired of being able to turn them from their constancy. He therefore decreed, in a final sentence, that they should be rounded up, and the slaughter completed. The troops sent to execute this order came to the blessed legion and drew their swords upon those holy men who, for love of life, did not refuse to die. They were all slain with the sword. They never resisted in any way. Putting aside their weapons, they offered their necks to the executioners. Neither their numbers nor the strength of arms tempted them to uphold the justice of their cause by force.

They kept just one thing in their minds: that they were bearing witness to Him who was led to death without protest, and who, like a lamb, opened not His mouth; but that now, they themselves, sheep in the Lord's flock, were to be massacred as it were by ravaging wolves. Thus, by the savage cruelty of this tyrant, that fellowship of the saints was perfected. For they despised things present in hope of things to come. So was slain that truly angelic legion of men who, we trust, now praise the Lord God of Hosts, together with the legions of angels, in Heaven forever.

Not all the members of the legion were at Aguanum at the time of the massacre. Others were posted along the military highway linking Switzerland with Germany and Italy. These were progressively and methodically martyred wherever they were found.... During their martyrdom, numerous miracles happened, which undoubtedly largely contributed to the massive conversion of the inhabitants of these regions to Christianity. In Zurich for instance, the three beheaded saints Felix, Regula and Exuperantius miraculously rose, carried their heads in their own hands, and walked to the top of a hill, where they knelt, prayed and at last lay down. On the same spot, a large cathedral was later erected. The three saints carrying their heads in their hands appear on the coat of arms and seal of Zurich until today.

Saints Victor, Orsus and their comrades were barbarously tortured by Hirtacus, the Roman governor of Solothurn. During this torture, several miracles occurred, e.g. the shackles suddenly broke open, the fire was instantaneously extinguished, etc. The lookers-on were thus filled with wonder and began to admire the Theban legionaires, upon which the furious Hirtacus ordered their immediate beheading. Without the slightest resistance they offered the executors their necks. The bodies of the beheaded Saints then shown in glaring brightness.

The bodies of the Saints which were thrown in the river Aar, advanced the bank, stepped out, walked heads on hands, then knelt and prayed at the spot where the Basilica of St. Peter later arose.[7]

Beloved, if we are blessed to join the heavenly company of martyrs, let's be really good ones that will cause the spectators to become believers! Believe God for the miraculous!

The Martyrs of Matanzas

Martyrs' blood was shed in Florida in the year 1564. French Protestants, called Huguenots, were being persecuted in France by Catholics. Gaspard de Coligny, the Admiral of the French fleet, was a Huguenot and he felt the only safe future for his people would be in the New World.

The Queen Mother, Catherine de Medici, considered colonizing the New World to be important for France, since Spain had been at it since Christopher Columbus set sail in 1492. Perhaps there really was gold that the French could exploit, as well as other commercial opportunities. And sending the Huguenots out of France would take the pressure off of the society. So in 1562, Captain Jean Ribault was sent to set up a colony.

He sailed up the St. John's River in present day Jacksonville, Florida. He called it the River of May, and dedicated the land there in the name of the king of France and set up a stone column as a testimony thereto. Then he sailed north to establish a Charlesfort in what is now Parris Island, South Carolina; however it didn't last long as a settlement.

On June 22, 1564, the French explorer René Goulaine de Laudonnière reached the coast of Florida and then

---

7   http://www.copticchurch.net/topics/synexarion/maurice.html (accessed 16 June 2019).

proceeded up the same waterway and landed to establish Fort Caroline. On June 30, he called for a feast to celebrate. The Timucua Indians warmly welcomed the French Huguenots and helped prepare a feast in their honor. "We sang a psalm of Thanksgiving unto God," Laudonnière wrote of the ensuing celebration, "beseeching Him that it would please His Grace to continue His accustomed goodness toward us."[8]

The Catholic King of Spain got wind of the French activities in what he considered Spanish Florida and sent Pedro Menéndez de Avilés with troops to defend his territory. His orders included wiping out the Protestants. He arrived around the same time as Jean Ribault who had come with supplies and more colonists.

They met at the mouth of the river and had an exchange of words and some shots. Then Menéndez sailed a few miles south to dedicate the land to the king of Spain, establishing St. Augustine on September 8, 1564.

Against the advice of Laudonnière, Ribault set out to perform a preemptive strike before the Spaniards could get settled. He was nearly successful, surprising the Spanish. However, the tide was out and they couldn't pass into the inlet. The next day a terrible storm came up and drove Ribault's ships aground in two different places.

Menéndez realized that if Ribault even survived the storm, he was too far away to help defend Fort Caroline, so he marched his troops north and captured the French Protestant settlement. The women and children were set aside for slavery.

Then, turning to the men, Menéndez called upon them to renounce their heresy and return to the bosom of the Catholic Church. If they refused, then they would suffer death. Two men among

---

8   http://www.jaxhistory.org/timucua_first_thanksgiving/ (acessed 16 June 2019).

the Huguenots did as Menéndez commanded and were spared. However, the rest remained firm in their Protestant convictions. Furthermore, they courageously replied: "We are in your power. You are master of our mortal bodies, but with the death before us that you threaten, know that we are members of the reformed Church of Christ, . . . that, holding it good to live in this faith, we deem it one in which it will not be amiss to die!"[9]

Ribault and his men who survived the shipwreck began to trudge north to return to Fort Caroline. Along the way, they reached Matanzas inlet and encountered Menéndez and his troops who told them of the fate of Fort Caroline.

The first contingent of around 150 sailors sought mercy from the Spanish but Menéndez was vague, promising them only whatever mercy God would direct of him. His "mercy" led to the slaughter of most, with only a handful of professed Catholics, artisans and musicians spared. Days later, Ribault and his men arrived at the very same spot. Charles Bennett records what happened next, on October 12, 1565, relying upon the deposition of a Spanish eyewitness for many details of this account.

Solis de Meras, a Spanish priest and eyewitness to the scene, described the massacre in the following words:

The Adelantado [Menéndez], taking Jean Ribault behind the sand hills, among the bushes where the others had their hands tied behind them, he said to these and all others as he had done before, that they had four leagues to go after night,

---

9   William Gilmore Simms, The Huguenots in Florida; or The Lily and the Totem (New York, 1854), p 361-362. Quoted on https://www.livetheadventureletter.com/education-history/fort-caroline-huguenot-settlement/ (accessed 17 June 2019).

and that he could not permit them to go unbound; and after they were all tied, he asked if they were Catholics or Lutherans, or if any of them desired to make confession...

The man who actually killed Ribault first inquired of him whether the French commander did not expect his soldiers to obey orders. Ribault answered, "Yes." Then the Spaniard said, "I propose to obey the orders of my commander also. I am ordered to kill you." The Psalm that Ribault recited before the dagger was thrust into his body was the 132nd Psalm which begins, "Lord, remember David"; but Ribault began it, according to an eyewitness, with "Lord, remember me."[10]

And so, America's first continuous European settlement, St. Augustine, was built with hands that had been stained with martyrs' blood. Later, many Huguenots came to America to find the liberty to worship and they helped to build this nation.

It is said that the blood of the martyrs is the seed of the Church. Perhaps it may also be understood that the blood of the martyrs of Fort Caroline and Matanzas was the seed of this nation, and that Liberty is bound to those who "love not their lives unto the death."[11]

It's not that persecution and martyrdom are intrinsically good, but as Paul pointed out in Romans 8:28, "And we know that **all things work together for good** to them that love God, to them who are the called according to His purpose." Then he goes on in verses 35-39:

---

10   Laudonniere & Fort Caroline: History and Documents, pp. 42-43: Quoted on http://virginiahuguenot.blogspot.com/2009/10/remember-me-o-lord.html (accessed 17 June 2019).

11   Revelation 12:11

Who shall separate us from the love of Christ? Shall tribulation, or distress, or persecution, or famine, or nakedness, or peril, or sword? As it is written, "For your sake we are killed all the day long; we are accounted as sheep for the slaughter." No, in all these things we are more than conquerors through Him that loved us. For I am persuaded, that neither death, nor life, nor angels, nor principalities, nor powers, nor things present, nor things to come, nor height, nor depth, nor any other creature, shall be able to separate us from the love of God, which is in Christ Jesus our Lord.

The grace of God is sufficient to keep us connected at the heart to the One Who loves us more than we can comprehend, even in the face of horrific adversity.

Chapter 10

The Born Loser

As a child I always enjoyed the comics section of the newspaper. At some point we can relate to how Charlie Brown felt when he would trust Lucy van Pelt one more time to hold the football for him to kick, even though every time before she had yanked the ball out of the way just as he arrived to kick it and he landed hard on his back.

How about Blondie's husband, Dagwood Bumstead. He's a little bit lazy, lying on the couch when he probably should be mowing the lawn. He's a little self-indulgent with his massive sandwiches. And he works for Mr. Dithers who berates and abuses him at every turn. Can't he do anything right?

Then there's Beetle Bailey, the lovable, generally insubordinate, and loafing army private. Sergeant Snorkel, better known as Sarge, has a temper with a short fuse. When Beetle mouths off or disobeys orders, the next panel shows a cloud of activity with fists, stars, and words like BAM! POW! SOK! Insults, profanity, and verbal abuse were displayed by something like # ✹ ✗ ⸮ ✱ ∂ ↄ # ! The panel following invariably had an unrecognizable heap the color of his uniform, with Beetle's bent arm, a shoe, a hand, a bare foot, and some mangled form of his head. Have you ever felt like that?

Then of course there's Brutus Thornapple, "The Born Loser," whose coat of arms in the title panel has a shield divided into quarters with pictures of a straight jacket, a tax return, a pair of glasses with one broken lens, and a poker hand that is one card short of a royal flush. The ribbon beneath the shield says, "HELP!" Nothing goes right for the poor guy and he's always being put down by his boss.

The perpetually dirty little kid, Pigpen, in the "Peanuts" comic strip, always had a cloud of dirt around him that he couldn't get rid of. He accepted his lot in life as "a dirt magnet."

Joe Btfsplk (yes, that's really how it is spelled) in "Li'l Abner" had a cloud of bad luck that was always raining over his head. Not only did nothing go right for him, but every time he showed up, something bad happened, even when everything was going right up to that point.

We find humor in their unfortunate situations, but perhaps it's because we resonate with them at times. These characters picture classic rejection.

Rejection Is Real

"All forms of perfectionism are linked to past experiences of rejection or unrealistic expectations. Perfectionists cope with some inner sadness or 'badness' by focusing on making their outer worlds beautiful and good."[1]

Wait a minute! Perfectionism? Uh-oh! That's me! That was my reaction when I understood this seed of truth. As I began to piece together the puzzle, I realized

---

1   https://teachinghumblehearts.com/en/toxic-effect-perfectionism/ (accessed 19 June 2019).

that my conception created some complications for my parents. My parents were missionaries. They were kind, good-hearted, godly people. When they were beginning to make preparations to return to the States after five years of service on the field, Mom wrote home to her parents giving the date of their sailing and arrival. In her next letter she said, "Well, I went to the gynecologist and she told me that we will have to delay our departure for home as I'm expecting."

So, imagine the excitement of the anticipated return to "normal" life in the States and the disappointment in the delay! Rejection! Then she wrote home about how the housing has become complicated because the family that is coming when they were supposed to have been gone will have no place to live because my coming has delayed their departure. It's all my fault! Rejection! If it weren't for me, everyone would be happy. I'm the cause of trouble.

She signed the last letter home before my arrival with all the family names: Ed, Elaine, Paul, John, Carole...and Henry. That's me. Henry. Only I can't be Henry—I'm a girl. Rejection! I'm not what they want me to be! The next communication was a telegram: "SHARON COOPER ARRIVED FOURTEENTH NIGHT EVERYTHING FINE CONGRATULATIONS." But they really wanted Henry, or so I thought.

All through my childhood I was a tomboy. I hated dressing in frills. I usually didn't want to play dolls with my sister, but when she got a Barbie, I got a Ken; then I would play. I really wanted to learn to play football with my older brothers. When the Detroit Tigers won the World Series in 1968, I wanted to learn to play baseball. I checked books out from the library on how to be a switch hitter and other baseball skills. Then I wanted to learn how to play basketball, etc., etc., etc.

In hindsight, I can see how the things we say over a baby in the womb can create a distorted mindset in the developing child. We did the same thing to my younger sister when she came along as a "late lamb" after I had been the baby of the family for nearly nine years. During the pregnancy we called the baby, "Nathan," but Christina Marie arrived instead. And sure enough, she was a tomboy too.

I hadn't learned this lesson when I was pregnant with our daughter. I was certain that I was going to have a boy and decided to call him Ian. I didn't want to have an ultrasound to reveal the baby's gender. Just two weeks before she was born, Carolyn Wright asked me what I was going to name the baby. "Ian," I said confidently.

"What if it's a girl?"

"It's going to be a boy."

"You'd better get a girl's name," she declared emphatically.

So I managed to narrow it down to a couple possibilities for a first name. When Heather was born, I certainly wasn't disappointed that she wasn't a boy—just puzzled. And my first words when I saw her were, "She's beautiful!" And she was! She was the prettiest baby I had ever seen! And I wasn't even being prejudiced! But sure enough, Heather didn't like to do girly stuff—she too was a tomboy.

I can't help but wonder if some of the gender questioning that is going around these days has its roots in a child's perceptions of words heard *in utero*. Words make a difference, even to a baby!

More Perceptions of Rejection

So when I was born and we eventually got back to the States, my mother at some point in my infancy announced to my dad, "I got up in the night with the first three. It's your turn." So unless there was a flu bug going through the house, if I woke up in the night, I went into my parents' room and tapped my dad on the arm saying, "Daddy, I had a dweam. Would you wock-a-bye me?"

I was happy with my dad taking care of me. But I didn't understand that a child is wired to feel safe and loved when her biological mother is nurturing her. Before I started school, my mother became a school teacher, leaving me with babysitters. Rejection!

Being the fourth child, I suppose I was the typical "pesky little sister," particularly to my two older brothers. I wanted to emulate them, especially when they were playing sports. They were six and seven years my elder, and I held them in high esteem. But why would two boys want their little sister hanging around? They were brilliant with puns and became experts in the art of sarcasm and put downs. Of course, striving for attention and being at the bottom of the pecking order, I received a lot "stiletto remarks" that cut deeply. Rejection!

When I started school I was a voracious learner. I had a tremendous appetite for knowledge and did very well in school. I excelled in almost everything I tried, and if I didn't excel in something new immediately, I'd give it up. I developed a pattern of "over compliance" and perfectionism. Perhaps I was trying to make myself acceptable so that I wouldn't be rejected.

I didn't realize until recently that four of the most significant memories I have of my mother, who passed away when I was thirteen, are of her embracing me at the approximate ages of 2 or 3, 6 or 7, and twice the last day I saw her.

Then the hollowness began. Everyone in the family was dealing with the pain of our loss. Abandonment. Emptiness. I was truly grateful for the Presence of the

Lord, as I had just received the Baptism of the Holy Spirit the week before Mom died. I was experiencing His comfort, but we learned in her absence how very much we depended on her to hold the family together. She was 43.

Racham

I don't know when I realized that I didn't feel loved. It's not that I wasn't loved. I could acknowledge it mentally. I heard people say, "I love you," and could feel love for people in my heart and I could show it and say it. But I couldn't feel it coming into me from them. It was like I had a Teflon coating on my heart and nothing would stick.

As I prayed about it, I had a revelation from the Lord. In Exodus 34, when Moses is on Mount Sinai to see the Lord's glory, He roared His name twice, then the first thing He declares to Moses about Himself was, "merciful." We need to dig a little deeper to understand what that really means. The Hebrew word is *rachum* (Strong's # H7349), meaning "compassionate." It is from the root word *racham* (Strong's #H7355), meaning "to sooth; to cherish; to love deeply like parents; to be compassionate... show pity, be tender; to have mercy... This verb usually refers to a strong love which is rooted in some kind of natural bond, often from a superior one to an inferior one.... Small babies evoke this feeling.... God looked upon His own people as a father looks upon his children; He has pity for them. He is gracious and merciful to whomever He chooses."[2]

One of the words that also has *racham* as its root is also pronounced *racham* and it means "a womb... the bowels [as the seat of emotions], compassion, mercy, sympathy, tenderness, pity, sensitive love."[3]

2   "Racham" Strong's H7355 definition from "Lexical Aids to the Old Testament" by Spiros Zodhiates, *Hebrew Greek Key Study Bible,* (c) 1984 and 1991 Spiros Zodhiates and AMG International, Inc. Chattanooga, TN

3   Ibid, "Racham" Strong's H7356

Can you see that the very first thing God reveals to Moses about Himself is that He has the compassion of a mother? When He made Adam in His image, it was before He separated Eve from Adam. Our Father has "womb mercies." He has the tender compassion of a mother soothing her small baby.

One morning as I was reaching out to God to heal the deficit I was feeling from my experience in the womb, I pulled myself into a fetal position and saw myself in the womb. Suddenly I experienced a flash of golden light that I understood to be our Father's *rachamim* (plural for *racham*) — His "womb mercies." That began a tremendous healing process that has been restoring my ability to feel loved. My emotions are being healed, glory to God!

I'm sure that many who will read this book have had much more devastating traumas than what I have just described. My point in sharing my experience is that the forever loser is constantly trying every means to do damage to us as early as possible to keep us from accomplishing our earthly assignment and negating his plans.

The Animal

One of the books that helped me formulate a lifestyle of praise and thanksgiving to the Lord is *Prison to Praise* by Merlin Carothers. In it he tells his testimony of losing his father at age twelve, leaving him angry with God and unhappy with life. He was training to be a paratrooper and was soon to enter World War II. In a moment of boredom, he stole a car and was apprehended by the FBI. His sentence was suspended so he could serve in the war. Later the Lord spoke to him that he had to make a decision to follow Him or it would be too late. As Carothers walked with Jesus through his life, he learned the life-changing key of keeping praise and thanksgiving in your heart and on your lips. He wrote this article that gives testimony of how transformative that can be.

"Here, Animal, read this!"

What should we do…with a man who is more animal than human?

Such a man was placed in one of our state prisons. He hated everyone, especially the guards. When ordered to do anything, he reacted in rage. Several guards were injured during his violent outbursts. Prison authorities really don't want inmates attacking their guards!

Each time the prisoner attacked someone, they put him in "The Hole." This was a slog underground cell – 8 feet by 8 feet. The solid concrete ceiling, walls and floor were 3 feet thick! The 16-foot-high ceiling was constructed of cement and steel. In the center of the ceiling there was a small door made of steel bars, and this was heavily bolted. No man has ever escaped from "The Hole."

The prisoner's entry into "The Hole" was without fanfare. Guards opened the ceiling door and lowered a ladder. The prisoner edged his way down into his hole and watched, no doubt with trepidation, as the ladder disappeared through the small square of light above him.

State laws had set the maximum stay in such total isolation at seven days per visit. Three times a day, guards lowered bread and water through the ceiling door and into the prisoner's hands.

For most men, the 7-day "treatment" was sufficient. From then on they usually followed the rules. But a guard told me that this prisoner seemed to have no control over his hatred for all men. When a guard told him to do anything, he would lash out at the guard with his fists, his feet or any weapon he could find. Within 24 hours of his being removed from "The Hole," he was again forced through the steel-barred door, and down into the cement tomb. There he bothered no one for another seven days.

After weeks and months of 7-day trips to this gruesome pit, the inmate became more like an animal than a man. He eventually was known as "The Animal."

One day the guard who was on duty had just finished reading my book, *Prison to Praise*. He thought, if any man ever needed this book, it's "The Animal." But he despised the prisoner so much that he didn't want to pick up the book, bend over and drop it through the steel bars. So he aimed his foot, kicked the book through the bars, and hollered, "Here, Animal, read this."

Alone, with nothing to do, the prisoner read Prison to Praise using the faint light that came between the steel bars 16 feet above him.

Later the prisoner told me what happened. As he read the book, he mocked everything I had written. He scoffed at the idea of thanking God for things that had happened to him. In derision and scorn he said, "OK, God, I thank you for that 3-foot-thick cement wall. . . .See, it's still there. Thanking you didn't do anything."

Item by item, the prisoner thanked God for each wall, the floor, the 16-foot-high ceiling and the steel-barred door. Laughing and mocking, he continued to challenge God. "Why don't you do something, God?" Then he thanked God for the damp coldness, the numerous cockroaches, his hunger pangs and his aching bones.

The prisoner told me that after exhausting his thankfulness for everything he could see, he thanked God for the guards that he hated, the prisoners who despised him, the judge who sentenced him, his worthless attorney, the witnesses who lied about him, the policemen who arrested him, the people who had kicked and beaten him when he was a boy and for his drunken, abusive parents. The list of people to hate seemed endless.

When "The Animal" finished his list, he went back and started all over. Hour after hour he laughed at God and dared Him to do something, anything-as he gave mocking praise and thanksgiving.

On the seventh day, the ladder was again lowered and the prisoner crawled out. The guard told me that he was totally flabbergasted when the man came through the trap door. He was smiling! He had never seen him smile. Even his eyes looked happy. He was a different man!

The prisoner told me what had happened. After days of thanking God, something had occurred that defies a natural explanation. A "Man" had appeared in his cell and said, "I love you," just those three words. "I knew it was true," 'The Animal' said. "His eyes were full of love for me."

The following hours were filled with genuine thanksgiving to God. The prisoner realized that he had waited his entire life to have that one moment with the Man he now knew to be Jesus!

The guard told me that the prisoner was a living miracle to behold. Instead of lashing out at people, he wanted to hug everyone! Gradually, the entire prison populace believed the man must have met with Jesus; he had miraculously become so much like Him!

Eventually the prisoner was released, pardoned by the governor, and became a prison chaplain. Why did Jesus appear to that man? He possibly knew Satan had such a hold on "The Animal" that there was no other way the man could be set free. I know that praising God has power! We never know what may happen when we are obedient to God's command. He said, "Give thanks always for all things, unto God and the Father in the name of Jesus Christ" (Ephesians 5:20). He also said, "All things work together for good to them that love God" (Romans 8:28).

Why doesn't Jesus appear in person to everyone who has a severe problem? I can't answer that. I know that He said, "It is best for you that I go away, for if I don't, the Comforter won't come" (John 16:7 TLB). It seems that for reasons unknown to us, most of us must go through difficult experiences in order to find our way to God.

Jesus told of the rich man who was in Hell. On earth he had so much wealth that he didn't know what to do with it all. The poor man, Lazarus, was covered in sores as he lay on the steps of the rich man's palace. "Now," Jesus said, "the rich man is in torment while Lazarus' joy is eternal." In some way Lazarus' suffering led him to God.

Jesus said it is difficult for a rich man to enter the Kingdom of Heaven. I believe that when He said "a rich man," He meant everyone who has an abundance of many good things. If we don't have problems, we don't seem to turn to God. Therefore, we often need problems.

In my first book, *Prison to Praise*, I told the story of how God clearly and dramatically convinced me that He wanted me to thank Him for everything that had ever happened to me. At first I couldn't understand how thanking Him for everything could do anything worthwhile. But He persisted, and eventually I began to understand.

As I continued to learn from Him, I wrote a second book, *Power in Praise*, in which I explained what I had learned.

As people read these two books, letters and phone calls came to me by the thousands. People told of an experiences as they practiced what I had written. Many of their encounters were as dramatic as that of "The Animal" who was visited by our Lord Jesus.

God will meet every man's and every woman's needs, in whatever way He knows to be right for that person. Jesus' promise was, "Come to Me, and I will give you rest" (Matthew 11:18).

You and I aren't in "The Hole," but we do have problems and needs. As we learn to believe that God is working for our good, we in a new way know and love His Son, Jesus.

There is indeed power in praising God, and it's a power that is available to everyone! [4]

Begin your journey into a new level of relationship with our loving Father with praise and thanks, and watch the healing and restoration begin!

---

4   https://www.apostolic.edu/here-animal-read-this/ (accessed 17 June 2019). Testimony used by permission.

Prison to Praise and *The Power of Praise* as well as "Here, Animal, Read This!" (in tract form) are all available on Merlin Carothers' website: http://www.foundationofpraise.org/

Chapter 11

The Real You

This sentence has a double meaning: "This battery is free of charge." In saying that, you might mean that this battery doesn't cost anything, but the person you said it to might understand that the battery isn't charged, so it has no power. In other words, a sentence with a double meaning can cause a misunderstanding.

The Bible has a number of statements that have a double meaning. In the third chapter of the book of John, Nicodemus, a member of the Sanhedrin (Council) came discreetly to visit Jesus in the night. He acknowledged that Jesus had to be from God because of the miracles that He was performing. Then Jesus tried to take him to a deeper level of understanding. The problem was, He used a statement with a double meaning.

Jesus made a statement that Nicodemus understood to mean, "You must be born again." What Jesus meant was, "You have to be engendered (fathered) from above." The translation from the Aramaic text is even clearer. You must be "'born from the origin.' The implication is that you must be born again like Adam was born by the direct breath of God. Nicodemus came seeking knowledge; Jesus offered him life."[1]

Jesus went on to talk about how the wind blows wherever it wants to, and so are they who are born or engendered by the Spirit (verses 7-8).

Every person is a spirit (Hebrew: *ruach* which also means breath) encased in a soul (Hebrew: *nephesh*). The soul is comprised of one's mind/intellect, will, and emotions. The soul is subject to temptation, with a weakness: a bent toward sin that has been passed from generation to generation beginning with the disobedience of Adam and Eve.

The spirit is basically like an unfertilized egg. It has life in the same way that our other cells are living, and it has the potential to be joined to a sperm and begin reproducing into a complete life.

The human spirit is waiting to be fertilized by the Holy Spirit. When that happens, it begins to grow, with the potential of becoming mature in the same way that a fertilized egg has the potential of becoming an adult. That's what Jesus was trying to explain to Nicodemus.

Until the Holy Spirit enters the human spirit, the soul is in charge. When the soul resists the prodding of the Holy Spirit, it becomes calloused, thicker and thicker, creating a hardened heart.[2] But when the human spirit receives the Breath of Life from our Father, just like Adam received the Breath of Life, our spirit comes alive within our soul with the ability to grow into a mature son of God.

1   Footnote from John 3:3 in The Passion Translation (TPT). https://www.biblegateway.com/passage/?search=john+3&version=TPT (accessed 18 June 2019).

2   John Paul Jackson. *Dreams and Mysteries.* https://www.youtube.com/watch?v=8e_dr7Fgxco&t=1389s Published 17 October 2014 (accessed 18 June 2019).

It's the soul that gets wounded by rejection and abuse. The intellect rises up and begins to question truth with the result that it is likely to accept lies as being plausible. Then the emotions kick in. Fear of being hurt stops us from loving and being loved, and the will steps in to say, "No, I won't accept that." Childish reasoning takes over and we are duped—snared!

So, even for the "born again" person, there's a war going on between the soul and spirit. The Apostle Paul wrote about it in his letter to the Romans, chapter seven. Brian Simmons has done a tremendous job bringing this scripture to life in The Passion Translation:

> When we were merely living natural lives,[3] the law, through defining sin, actually awakened sinful desires within us, which resulted in bearing the fruit of death. But now that we have been fully released from the power of the law, we are dead to what once controlled us. And our lives are no longer motivated by the obsolete way of following the written code,[4] so that now we may serve God by living in the freshness of a new life in the power of the Holy Spirit.[5]

The Purpose of the Law

So, what shall we say about all this? Am I suggesting that the law is sinful? Of course not! In fact, it was the law that gave us the clear definition of sin. For example, when the law said, "Do not covet,"[6] it became the catalyst to see how wrong it was for me to crave what belongs to someone else. It was through God's commandment that sin was

---

3   Romans 7:5 That is, before we came to know Jesus Christ.

4   Romans 7:6 Or "the oldness of the letter."

5   Romans 7:6 Or "by a new, Holy Spirit-empowered life."

6   Romans 7:7 See Ex. 20:17; Deut. 5:21.

awakened in me and built its base of operation[7] within me to stir up every kind of wrong desire. For in the absence of the law, sin hides dormant.[8] I once lived without a clear understanding of the law, but when I heard God's commandments, sin sprang to life and brought with it a death sentence. The commandment that was intended to bring life brought me death instead. Sin, by means of the commandment, built a base of operation within me, to overpower me[9] and put me to death. So then, we have to conclude that the problem is not with the law itself, for the law is holy and its commandments are correct and for our good.

So, did something meant to be good become death to me? Certainly not! It was not the law but sin unmasked that produced my spiritual death. The sacred commandment merely uncovered the evil of sin so it could be seen for what it is. For we know that the law is divinely inspired and comes from the spiritual realm,[10] but I am a human being made of flesh and trafficked as a slave under sin's authority.[11]

I'm a mystery to myself,[12] for I want to do what is right, but end up doing what my moral

7   Romans 7:8 Or "a starting point."

8   Romans 7:8 Or "is lifeless."

9   Romans 7:11 Or "deceive me" or "lead me astray."

10   Romans 7:14 Or "is spiritual."

11   Romans 7:14 Or "sold and ruined under sin." The Greek word *piprasko* refers to a slave who is "sold for exportation, betrayed and ruined."

12   Romans 7:15 Paul's use of "I" is most likely his identification with the people of Israel under the law prior to receiving Christ. It is not merely an autobiographical statement that Paul experienced all of these things, but a rhetorical device of solidarity with the experience of those who live under the law. Romans ch. 7 is not the present experience of any one person, but the testimony of a delivered person describing the condition of an undelivered one.

instincts condemn. And if my behavior is not in line with my desire, my conscience still confirms the excellence of the law. **And now I realize that it is no longer my true self doing it, but the unwelcome intruder of sin in my humanity.** For I know that nothing good lives within the flesh of my fallen humanity. The longings to do what is right are within me, but will-power is not enough to accomplish it.[13] My lofty desires to do what is good are dashed when I do the things I want to avoid. So if my behavior contradicts my desires to do good, I must conclude that **it's not my true identity doing it, but the unwelcome intruder of sin hindering me from being who I really am.**

Through my experience of this principle, I discover that even when I want to do good, evil is ready to sabotage me. **Truly, deep within my true identity, I love to do what pleases God.** But I discern another power operating in my humanity, waging a war against the moral principles of my conscience[14] and bringing me into captivity as a prisoner to the "law" of sin—this unwelcome intruder in my humanity. What an agonizing situation I am in! So who has the power to rescue this miserable man from the unwelcome intruder of sin and death?[15] I give all my thanks to God, for His mighty power has finally provided a way out through our Lord Jesus, the Anointed One! So if left to myself, the flesh is aligned with

---

13 Romans 7:18 Some Greek manuscripts have "but I don't know how to do it."

14 Romans 7:23 As translated from the Aramaic. The Greek is "warring against the law of my mind."

15 Romans 7:24 Or "Who will free me from this body of death?"

the law of sin, but now my renewed mind is fixed on and submitted to God's righteous principles.[16]

Romans 8

So now the case is closed. There remains no accusing voice of condemnation against those who are joined in life-union with Jesus, the Anointed One.[17] For the "law" of the Spirit of life flowing through the anointing of Jesus has liberated us[18] from the "law" of sin and death. For God achieved what the law was unable to accomplish, because the law was limited by the weakness of human nature.[19]

Yet God sent us His Son in human form to identify with human weakness. Clothed with humanity, God's Son gave His body to be the sin-offering so that God could once and for all condemn the guilt and power of sin. So now every righteous requirement of the law can be fulfilled through the Anointed One living His life in us. And we are free to live, not according to our flesh, but by the dynamic power of the Holy Spirit![20] [21]

16   Romans 7:25 Or "God's law."

17   Romans 8:1 Or "Those who are in Christ Jesus cannot be condemned." Although there are some manuscripts that add to this verse, "for those who do not walk according to the flesh but according to the Spirit," the addition is not supported by the oldest and most reliable Greek manuscripts.

18   Romans 8:2 Some Greek manuscripts have "sets me free" or "sets you [singular] free."

19   Romans 8:3 Or "weakness of the flesh."

20   Romans 8:4 What joyous truths are found in Rom. 8! All that God requires of us has been satisfied by the sacrifice of Jesus Christ. The life of Jesus in us is enough to satisfy God. The power of our new life is not the works of our weak humanity, but the dynamic power of the Holy Spirit released in us.

21   Romans 7:5-8:4 The Passion Translation (TPT) https://www.biblegateway.com/passage/?search=Romans+7&version=TPT and https://www.biblegateway.com/passage/?search=Romans+8&version=TPT (accessed 18 June 2019).

The Spirit

In his book, *The Spiritual Man*, Watchman Nee gives this Analysis of the Spirit:

The human spirit is comprised of:

1 The intuition

2 Communion (with God)

3 The conscience

In the war that wages within us, when we allow the Holy Spirit to rule in our lives, our intuition will answer our intellect, silencing our carnal reasonings.

Our communion (fellowship) with the Lord will answer our emotions. His *shalom*—His peace will still "the storm in our water glass."

Proverbs 20:27 says, "The spirit of man is the lamp of the LORD, Searching all the inward parts."[22] This lamp of the Lord is our conscience and it steps up to answer our will when it is out of line.

When we give our spirit that has been fertilized by the Spirit-Breath of our Father a higher priority than our soul, everything in our body comes into order. And when we truly learn to walk in the Spirit, our intellect and our emotions will be in submission to our God-united spirit. We will have laid down our will to take up the will of God.

"For all who are led by the Spirit of God are sons of God" (Romans 8:14 AMPC). The word in Greek for "sons" in this scripture is *huios* (pronounced yos), Strong's #5207. It means:

Son, distinguished from *teknon* (5043), child... *huios* is reserved for the Son of God. *Huios* primarily signifies the relation of offspring to parent and

---

22 Provers 20:27. JPS Tanakh 1917. https://biblehub.com/proverbs/20-27.htm (accessed 18 June 2019).

not simply the birth as indicated by *teknon*. Used metaphorically of prominent moral characteristics...; legitimate offspring; descendants, irrespective of their gender; generally demonstrating behavior or character... The difference between believers as children (*tekna*) of God and as sons (*huioi*) is brought out in Romans 8:14-21. *Tekna* refers to those who were born of God and *huioi* refers to those who show maturity acting as sons.... *Huios* gives evidence of the dignity of one's relationship and likeness to God's character.[23]

Huios[5207] is also used in Hebrews 12:5-11.

"And you have forgotten the exhortation which speaks unto you as unto children,[5207] My son,[5207] despise not you the chastening of the Lord, nor faint when you are rebuked of Him: **For whom the Lord loves He chastens, and scourges every son**[5207] **whom He receives. If you endure chastening, God deals with you as with sons;**[5207] **for what son**[5207] **is he whom the father chastens not?** But if you be without chastisement, whereof all are partakers, then are you bastards, and not sons.[5207] Furthermore we have had fathers of our flesh which corrected us, and we gave them reverence: **shall we not much rather be in subjection unto the *Father of spirits*, and live?** For they verily for a few days chastened us after their own pleasure; but He for our profit, that we might be partakers of His holiness. **Now no chastening for the present seems to be joyous, but grievous: nevertheless afterward it yields the peaceable fruit of righteousness unto them which are exercised thereby.**"

23 "Huios" Strong's G5207 definition from "Lexical Aids to the New Testament" by Spiros Zodhiates, *Hebrew Greek Key Study Bible*, (c) 1984 and 1991 Spiros Zodhiates and AMG International, Inc. Chattanooga, TN

Some of the things we suffer through are meant for our instruction and development as mature "sons." Ultimately, our Father's goal is for us to grow up and join Him in His "Family Business." Can't you just imagine: "God and Sons, Wonder-Working Company"!

Learning to receive correction graciously is a sign of maturity. Don and Catherine James teach that another sign of maturity is seen by how fast you get up and get back into the race when you have stumbled or fallen.

The accuser (forever loser) tries to wear down the saints, pushing, prodding, cajoling, tempting until the person falls into his snare. Then he changes tactics and pours slimy shame on, hoping to keep the person from repenting. "Look at what you did! Just look at how terrible you are! God won't want you now! You've sullied His reputation by doing that! Just give up! He'll never want you back!" Of course all of that is a lie—run to our Father! He's waiting for your return.

Peter's Denial

The following is from my journal, recorded in November 2003.

"Then took they Him, and led Him, and brought Him into the high priest's house. And Peter followed afar off. And when they had kindled a fire in the midst of the hall, and were set down together, Peter sat down among them. But a certain maid beheld him as he sat by the fire, and earnestly looked upon him, and said, This man was also with Him. And he denied Him, saying, Woman, I know Him not. And after a little while another saw him, and said, You are also of them. And Peter said, Man, I am not. And about the space of one hour after another confidently affirmed, saying, Of a truth this fellow also was with Him: for he is a Galilaean. And

Peter said, Man, I know not what you say. And immediately, while he yet spoke, the cock crowed. And the Lord turned, and looked upon Peter. And Peter remembered the word of the Lord, how He had said unto him, Before the cock crows, you shalt deny Me three times. And Peter went out, and wept bitterly" (Luke 22:54-62).

"... I know Him not..." verse 57b.

KNOW (Strong's Concordance #1492) "... to perceive with the senses... sight... mind.... intuitively."

This was the same man who had declared "You are the Christ, the Son of the living God!" And I had told him that flesh and blood had not revealed it to him, but My Father in Heaven (Mt. 16:16-17).

Peter knew! He knew Who I was by the knowing of the Spirit—in his "knower." He was totally confident of Who I was and that confidence made him reply to My question, "Will you also go away?" with:

"Lord, to whom shall we go? You have the words of eternal life. And we believe and are sure that You are that Christ, the Son of the living God" (John 6:66-69).

It was upon this knowledge that is deeper than experience that I intended to build My Church. But Peter was being sifted like wheat (Luke 22:31). He was experiencing the shaking that separates the chaff from the grain. It is the shaking of all that can be shaken, so that that which cannot be shaken will remain (Hebrews 12:27).

Peter needed to "be converted" from a mixture of chaff and wheat to bare, naked grain that could

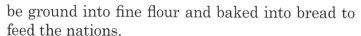

be ground into fine flour and baked into bread to feed the nations.

The servant is not greater than his Master (John 15:20). I too was enduring the shaking of My life at that time. No human could be there for Me to lean on. I had to walk this out alone for you—so that when you walk through your shakings, you'll know I went through them first for you, and you'll be able to lean on Me, alone, for I will not leave you alone.

Peter was shaken so that when he repented of his natural instinct for self-preservation, he would have the "bare necessities" he needed to be able to strengthen his brethren!

The chaff is the outer, protective covering of the grain. It is in the carnal nature of fallen man to cling to the protection that kept him safe during his nurtured growing season. But when it is time to move into a new level, you must be willing to be stripped of that protection if you want to be "bread" for the nations.

I endured My shaking and My stripping so that I could be the Bread of Life for you. I have called you to be like Me, your Master. What I suffered, you can also endure because I went there first and paved the way. If the world hated Me, it will also hate you. But if the common people heard Me gladly, they will also hear you.

Don't be afraid of the siftings that are yet ahead. See them as good. I have prayed for you and My grace is sufficient for you. Fear only torments and binds you from doing My will and being what I destined you to be. Let go of the shoreline. Loose yourself from the pier that would destroy you in the storm. Launch out into the deep and trust Me that I have been there before you to prepare your way. (You are no longer a little boat!)

Peter knew what it was like to "step out of the boat" to walk to Me even on a boisterous sea. He had first hand experience with knowing My power to save him from his own fearful perceptions.

He knew I was the Lord of Life, but when I stood in the "judgment," he couldn't see that I could have the power over My own death.

It is very difficult to overcome the fear of death, but unless you do, you will all your life be subject to bondage (Hebrews 2:15). You must trust Me to be with you as you die daily. As I overcame the power of death, I will give you the strength to overcome as well.

Die to your ambitions. I have a greater vision for you. TRUST ME! I am gentle even when the shaking becomes severe.

When I looked at Peter in the moment of the crowing of the cock, it was a look of truth, not condemnation. He was grieved by the recognition of his own weakness. He wept bitterly because he found out that he was only a "rock" when he was walking in right standing with Me. He knew his denial of Me had momentarily saved his neck, but now his very soul was in peril. He had found out that all his personal strength and bravado were only wind in the face of death. Once his "cover was blown," he discovered the naked truth about himself. The chaff (the façade) was stripped from him and he found himself to truly be a coward and very alone.

He was tormented by the accuser of the brethren. The same one who had pushed him into the corner, drawing his "flesh" into the ring, now viciously poured guilt into his fresh "flesh wounds."

When these things happen to you, know that I allow them to show you the truth about your own carnal nature. They are "only" flesh wounds, and I will turn them into jewels to be displayed for eternity.

If I don't allow your carnal nature to be exposed, you will never overcome it! I'm looking for overcomers! Learn that I give you the shakings for your own good, your own growth!

The enemy of your soul hates you passionately and desires to bring you evil, trauma and torment. But he cannot do to you what I do not permit.

I love you to your very depths with a passionate, everlasting love and I will never leave you nor forsake you. I walk with you through your shakings. I was even with Peter when he was trying from his innermost being to be there for Me, but his instinct for self-preservation kept trying to tug his "security blanket" of chaff around him. Flesh can never really protect you.

Understand that although the shakings appear to bring out the flesh in you, the real purpose is to make that flesh covering split and peel off to expose the real you that I have sanctified. And that real you is food in My hands that I will use to feed the poor and needy lambs and sheep who are hungry for something real.

You know what it's like to take a bite of a whole grain food (bread, oatmeal, rice) and find a piece of hull (chaff). You want to spit it out. Understand that My shakings and siftings are for the purpose of making you "palatable" to the nations. You will never have to go through them alone, for when you are being shaken, I am on trial as well. Your response (even if you fall and repent) shows whether "I Am that I Am" or not!

Chapter 12
Why?

We know that Job's sufferings were completely unwarranted from an earthly perspective. From a heavenly perspective, it was as though the adversary, the forever loser, had filed a suit to gain permission to test Job, but God's plans were bigger and better than that. So the reason in that case was that God wanted to reveal Himself to Job in the whirlwind. He wanted to increase Job's understanding of His greatness. Even though he was not known as a proud man, Job was humbled by the experience, having had too small of an opinion of God.

Sin Opens Doors

Sometimes, however, our sufferings have earthly, fleshly causes. The Bible is clear about reaping what we sow. If we sow to flesh, we will reap corruption (Galatians 6:7-8), and if you sow wickedness, you will reap the same (Job 4:8).

The Lord is the God of all flesh (Jeremiah 32:27). When we are rightly related to Him, we dwell under His shadow. It's like a big umbrella that keeps the rain of trouble off of us. But when we rebel against His ways, we step out from underneath His protection, and we suffer the consequences.

"Flesh Flash"

Sometimes we have a "flesh flash," and the carnal nature overtakes our best intentions. HALT is an acronym for the times when we are the most vulnerable: When we are HUNGRY, ANGRY, LONELY, and TIRED. I've come to the conclusion that we need to add when you are sick or in pain to that list. You can take a lot and keep your attitude right when you're not in pain, but when you are in pain it is much harder! It is much more difficult to stay connected to the Lord in any of those times, and we are the most likely to lash out in one of these moments of weakness when pressure is applied.

If we don't repent, that is, turn back to God, ask His forgiveness for our error, receive His cleansing, and line up with His way, the trouble will only perpetuate. It will be like a seed planted that will bear fruit. But repentance and cleansing draws on the mercy of God, relying on Jesus having paid the penalty for our sin. Absolute freedom belongs to us at that point! However, the father of lies will continue to slime us with shame, if he can get us to buy his lie that we are still responsible for paying for our error. It is true that if we harmed another person in the process of our error, that we owe a heartfelt apology and perhaps restitution, but when God forgives, we are clear.

When I Cause the Wound

This is a favorite story that was going around in email some years ago. It is posted on many websites as a very important lesson for life. We have to take responsibility for our "flesh flashes"!

There once was a little boy who had a bad temper. His father gave him a bag of nails and told him that every time he lost his temper, he must hammer a nail into the back of the fence.

The first day the boy had driven 37 nails into the fence. Over the next few weeks, as he learned to control his anger, the number of nails hammered daily gradually dwindled down. He discovered it was easier to hold his temper than to drive those nails into the fence.

Finally the day came when the boy didn't lose his temper at all. He told his father about it and the father suggested that the boy now pull out one nail for each day that he was able to hold his temper. The days passed and the young boy was finally able to tell his father that all the nails were gone.

The father took his son by the hand and led him to the fence. He said, "You have done well, my son, but look at the holes in the fence. The fence will never be the same. When you say things in anger, they leave a scar just like this one. You can put a knife in a man and draw it out. It won't matter how many times you say I'm sorry, the wound is still there."

The little boy then understood how powerful his words were. He looked up at his father and said "I hope you can forgive me father for the holes I put in you."

"Of course I can," said the father.[1]

Pride

One of the greatest and most insidious weapons that the adversary uses to bring accusation against us is pride.

---

1   Author Unknown. Nails In The Fence. http://www.inspirationpeak.com/cgi-bin/ stories.cgi?record=50 (accessed 24 June 2019).

He knows that it will make God resist us and distance Himself from us.[2]

Daniel chapter 4 and 5:18-21 describes how Nebuchadnezzar's heart was lifted up, and his mind was hardened in pride. As a consequence, he was deposed from his kingly throne, and his glory was taken from him. He spent seven years eating grass like an animal, living outside where the dew fell on him at night. His hair grew and became like feathers, and his nails grew like birds' claws. His heart was changed from a man's to a beast's, until he learned that God's kingdom rules—not his kingdom, and not him! His mind returned at that point and he resumed his royal duties as a much humbler man.

When Moses came to Pharaoh to demand, "Let my people go," we read that God hardened his heart. Now you may think that's not fair! But the Hebrew word gives us the understanding that God "strengthened" his heart. In other words, Pharaoh's heart was already hard and proud. All God did was strengthen what was already there.

The Hebrew word, *Rahav* (*Rahab*) means "fierceness, insolence, pride, and is a poetical name for Egypt."[3] The king of Egypt was the epitome of pride and insolence, and God didn't take kindly to this fierce nation enslaving His Chosen people. But if they hadn't been enslaved, they would never have cried out to God to deliver them from

---

2   James 4:6b, "Wherefore he saith, God resists the proud, but gives grace unto the humble."

Psalm 138:6, "Though the Lord be high, yet has He respect unto the lowly: but the proud He knows afar off."

Psalm 101:5b, "Him that has an high look and a proud heart will not I suffer."

Proverbs 16:5, "Every one that is proud in heart is an abomination to the Lord: though hand join in hand, he shall not be unpunished."

3   "*Rahab*" Strong's #H7293. *Gesinius' Hebrew Chaldee Lexicon.* https://www.blueletterbible.org/lang/lexicon/lexicon.cfm?Strongs=H7293&t=KJV (accessed 20 June 2019).

Rich Wounds

Egypt, so they never would have made it to the Promised Land! His ways are higher than our ways!

We can learn a lesson from this: recognize that pride keeps you in bondage as a slave, and crying out to God for deliverance will pour retribution on the demonic or fleshly slave driver so you can be liberated.

Pride has devastating results. Just look at the future of the king of pride: "Your heart was lifted up because of your beauty, you have corrupted your wisdom by reason of your brightness: **I will cast you to the ground, I will lay you before kings, that they may behold you**" (Ezekiel 28:17). And:

"How are you **fallen from heaven, O Lucifer, son of the morning! how are you cut down to the ground,** which didst weaken the nations! For you have said in your heart, I will ascend into heaven, I will exalt my throne above the stars of God: I will sit also upon the mount of the congregation, in the sides of the north: I will ascend above the heights of the clouds; I will be like the most High. **Yet you shalt be brought down to hell, to the sides of the pit. They that see you shall narrowly look upon you, and consider you, saying, Is this the man that made the earth to tremble, that did shake kingdoms**" (Isaiah 14:12-16).

It is wisdom to ask the Holy Spirit to reveal pride in our hearts. Sometimes we might find pride to be the root of embarrassment. Pride can cause us to lie to prevent us from having to confess a mistake we made. Pride can cause us to keep our true feelings hidden when we've been offended, thus preventing a person from apologizing when they don't know they've hurt you. The accuser of the brethren is always busy trying to separate people from each other.

Now we all want to be humble, but if we don't humble ourselves, our loving Heavenly Father will see to it that we get there by humiliation. He doesn't want to do it that way. He would rather that we humble ourselves, but He doesn't want us to face the consequences of the sin of pride, so He'll allow us to be humiliated for our good.

Many Other Sins

Deuteronomy 27 and 28 spell out numerous causes of curses such as holding your parents in contempt, moving a landmark, allowing the blind to wander, perverting judgment for the stranger, widow, or fatherless, etc. The blessings are spelled out for those who observe all of God's commandments, and curses for those who don't serve Him with gladness.

Romans 6:23 declares, "For the wages of sin is death; but the gift of God is eternal life through Jesus Christ our Lord." Every kind of sin leads to death and suffering on the way there. Thank God that repentance and the cleansing power of the Blood of Jesus sets us free from that.

God specifies that there are certain sins, though, that not only cause us to suffer personally by getting out from under His umbrella, they will also bring a curse on the land. Let's look at four primary ones:

Shedding of Innocent Blood

The shedding of innocent blood brings a curse on both land and people. Numbers 35:33 says, "So you shall not pollute the land wherein you are: for **blood it defiles the land:** and the land cannot be cleansed of the blood that is shed therein, but by the blood of him that shed it."

That means that manslaughter and murder bring corruption and defilement on the land. Of course, this includes the shedding of the blood of innocent babies in the womb.

Thankfully, the Lord made provision for unsolved murders in Deuteronomy 21. Because the blood of the innocent could only be atoned for by the blood of the murderer, in a case where the murderer could not be found, the Lord provided the substitution of the blood of a heifer to prevent the defilement of the land. In the same way, the Blood of Jesus now atones for our sins, including innocent bloodshed.[4]

Sexual Immorality

The Bible is very specific in spelling out what God considers immoral sexual activity. Leviticus chapter 18 goes into the details. In the King James Version and several others, the expression used is "uncover.. nakedness." It is translated "to have sexual relations" in the NIV, NLT, BSB, ISV, or "sexual intercourse" in the CSB, MET, HCSB. But if you go back to the Hebrew, it could also be translated "to make bare the genitals." This opens the understanding to include that other manners of lewdness and petting without penetration also disgust God. This passage forbids these acts to a man and:

- his father or mother
- his stepmother
- his sister or half-sister
- his granddaughter
- his step-granddaughter
- his paternal aunt
- his maternal aunt
- his paternal uncle or his wife
- his daughter-in-law
- his sister-in-law
- a woman and her daughter or granddaughter

---

4   Once you have dealt with your own sin history and that of your bloodline, study Gwen Shaw's book, *Redeeming the Land,* Engeltal Press.

- sisters as wives at the same time
- a woman on her period

He is also forbidden to:

- have sexual relations with a neighbor's wife (adultery)
- sacrifice his child to Molech (a foreign god)
- profane the name of Yehovah
- lie with a man as with a woman (homosexuality)
- lie with a beast (bestiality—this also applies to women)

After listing all these things, God says,

Defile not you yourselves in any of these things: for in all these the nations are defiled which I cast out before you: And the land is defiled: therefore I do visit the iniquity thereof upon it, and the land itself vomits out her inhabitants. You shall therefore keep My statutes and My judgments, and **shall not commit any of these abominations**; neither any of your own nation, nor any stranger that sojourns among you: (For all these abominations have the men of the land done, which were before you, and the land is defiled;) **That the land spue not you out also, when you defile it, as it spued out the nations that were before you.** For whosoever shall commit any of these abominations, even the souls that commit them shall be cut off from among their people. Therefore shall you keep mine ordinance, **that you commit not any one of these abominable customs**, which were committed before you, and that you **defile not yourselves therein**: I am the Lord your God.

So you can see how sexual immorality opens the door to evil. Howard Pittman in his book, *Demons, An Eyewitness*

Account explains that the lowest rank of demons are the ones associated with lust, perversion, and sexual immorality. The other demons find them despicable, but they are door openers to other demons.[5] In other words, if they can get you to sin sexually, a demon of lust can come in and make the way for others to join him.

Sexual sin not only defiles the individuals involved, Leviticus 18:25 shows that it actually defiles the land. When the land is defiled, the people living in it come under the curse of that defilement. It can cause a darkness that dulls the spiritual senses and lulls good people into a spiritual stupor and welcomes evil ones to perpetuate more evil. This sin has far-reaching implications and the adversary tries to use it to take full advantage to capture whole lands and people groups.

When sexual immorality ensnares a church leader, it's not unusual for it to spread to the pews, defiling the whole congregation. Those who practice witchcraft and sorcery are busy fasting, chanting, and doing incantations to bring this to pass. Intercessors need to step up to pray for pastors to be protected, and the pastors must live circumspectly with a healthy devotional relationship with the Lord in order to be able to overcome through the power and authority of the Blood of Jesus.

Occult Practices

One of the reasons that satanic ritual abuse includes sexual molestation is the way that it opens the door to other evil. God calls these things an abomination. That means that He finds them utterly disgusting! At the top of the list of people not allowed in God's Holy Land[6] is one who would cause his son or daughter to pass through the fire, referring to making a sacrifice to Molech. Next are:

5   Pittman, Howard O. *Demons, An Eyewitness Account.* (Philadelphian Publishing House:Foxworth, 1995).

6   Found in Deuteronomy 18:9-12.

- those who practice divination,
- an "observer of times," that is, soothsayer, enchanter, sorceress, diviner, fortune teller,[7]
- an enchanter, one who whispers (a magical spell), practices sorcery, gives oracles, prognosticates,[8]
- a witch,
- a charmer, one who casts spells or ties magic knots,[9]
- a consulter with familiar spirits,
- a wizard, magician, sorcerer,[10]
- a necromancer, one who consults with the dead or serves *Mot* the Canaanite god of the dead.[11]

Practicing these dark arts is so disgusting to God that it will cause the Land to actually cast the people out of it. Allowing witchcraft, etc., causes the suffering of the loss of inheritance as well as all the evil and perversion it produces.

Idolatry

An evil akin to witchcraft and sorcery is idolatry.[12] God declares it to also be abominable (disgusting, detestable).[13] Do you see how sexual abomination is linked to others? Sexual abuse is in witchcraft, and it is

---

7   "*Anan,*" *Blue Letter Bible* Strong's #H6046, https://www.blueletterbible.org/lang/lexicon/lexicon.cfm?Strongs=H6049&t=KJV (accessed 19 June 2019).

8   "*Nachash,*" Strong's H5172 definition from "Lexical Aids to the Old Testament" by Spiros Zodhiates, *Hebrew Greek Key Study Bible,* (c) 1984 and 1991 Spiros Zodhiates and AMG International, Inc. Chattanooga, TN

9   Ibid. "*chever*" Strong's #H2267.

10   Ibid. "*yidd°oni*" Strong's #H3049.

11   Ibid. "*Mot*" Strong's #H4191.

12   Isaiah 19:3 "And the spirit of Egypt shall fail in the midst thereof; and I will destroy the counsel thereof: and they shall seek to the idols, and to the charmers, and to them that have familiar spirits, and to the wizards."

13   2 Kings 23:24 KJV "Moreover the workers with familiar spirits, and the wizards, and the images, and the idols, and all the abominations that were spied in the land of Judah

also found in idolatry. Many of the Canaanite and other neighboring people groups around Israel were given to worshipping fertility gods. They had the mistaken idea that in order for their sowing of seeds to produce bountiful crops, they had to plant their personal seed in the temple prostitute.[14] It's no wonder that God called idolatry adultery! They were literally breaking their marriage covenants with their wives as well as breaking their covenant with the Almighty to worship other gods. Jeremiah 3:1-2, 9 indicates that this pollutes and defiles the land.

The first two of the ten commandments are:

1) You shalt have **no other gods** before Me.

2) You shalt not make unto you any **graven image**, or any likeness of any thing that is in heaven above, or that is in the earth beneath, or that is in the water under the earth: **You shalt not bow down thyself to them, nor serve them:** for I the LORD your God am a jealous God, **visiting the iniquity of the fathers upon the children unto the third and fourth generation** of them that hate Me; And shewing mercy unto thousands of them that love Me, and keep My commandments. (Exodus 20:3-6)

Leviticus 26:1 not only forbids idols and graven images, it also prohibits raising up "standing stones" or stones with an image on them. Included in the definition of standing stones would be an obelisk (a phallic symbol) the likes of Stonehenge. God detests these things.

---

and in Jerusalem, did Josiah put away, that he might perform the words of the law which were written in the book that Hilkiah the priest found in the house of the LORD."

14   http://bibleresources.americanbible.org/resource/prostitution-in-the-bible (accessed 20 June 2019) and Jeremiah 3:1-2.

Generational Iniquity

Once we have dealt with our own personal sins, much of the trouble we experience comes from sins going back to the third and fourth generation. Iniquities that weren't dealt with by the person who committed them come down the family line as potential problems. Addictive behaviours, abuse, negligence, violence, evil practices, etc., are passed along in the DNA to create weaknesses. But just because a predisposition has been passed on to you, doesn't mean that you have to give in to it. Many with alcoholic parents, for instance, have stopped the cycle without succumbing to it.

Anchoring your soul on the Word of God with the help of the Holy Spirit, will set you on a path to victory.

Unforgiveness

Another extremely potent tactic of the forever loser is to cause an offense that is "unforgivable." It's not really true that it's unforgivable, but we can be so hurt or devastated that forgiving becomes very difficult. And the accuser is right there supplying all the reasons not to forgive. He knows that if he can keep us from forgiving, he can take us to Hell with him—that's his highest goal!

Jesus made it very clear that if you don't forgive, you won't be forgiven:

"For if you forgive men their trespasses, your heavenly Father will also forgive you: **But if you forgive not men their trespasses, neither will your Father forgive your trespasses**" (Matthew 6:14-15).

Jesus told a parable of king who forgave his servant an enormous debt because he begged for mercy, not having the ability to pay. Then that servant refused to forgive a small debt of his fellow servant. The king angrily threw him in debtor's prison because he hadn't extended the mercy he had received—so he lost that mercy! Jesus ends the parable by saying, "So likewise shall My heavenly Father do also unto you, if you **from your hearts** forgive not every one his brother their trespasses" (Matthew 18:35).

"And when you stand praying, **forgive**, if you have ought against any: **that your Father also which is in heaven may forgive you your trespasses**" (Mark 11:25).

"**But if you do not forgive, neither will your Father which is in heaven forgive your trespasses**" (Mark 11:26).

A friend of mine told the story of how she had a fight with her husband. She was angry and stomped away to the bedroom, crying out to God for His help with her stubborn husband. The Lord said to her, "You must forgive him."

"What? After the way he spoke to me?"

"If you want Me to forgive you, you have to forgive him."

So, reluctantly, she returned to the living room to her husband. Half-heartedly she said, "I forgive you."

He laughed and said, "I forgive you too."

This infuriated her the more and she stomped back to the bedroom. Then she told the Lord, "There! I forgave him."

"And I forgive you in the same measure you forgave him!"

Needless to say, my friend truly repented and forgave her husband.

Laurie Ditto shares her testimony that she was worshipping the Lord in a service in the International House of Prayer in Kansas City when she suddenly found herself in Hell and saw other Christians there. She was

141

told, "You are in Hell eternally for unforgiveness." She described it as being worse than any words she could come up with. The extreme heat caused her skin to begin to drip off her. The screams of the damned were so loud and horrible that it caused her pain. She knew that this was going to go on eternally. "The pain was excruciating. There's no relief, no water, no light."

There were people there who believed that Jesus is Lord, but they refused to obey Him. She knew that the scriptures taught that if you love the Lord, you'll obey Him, but she wouldn't obey—she wouldn't forgive. She realized that compared to all the Lord was willing to forgive her of, these offenses she hadn't been able to let go of were small.

Then, as suddenly as she had been taken to Hell, she was brought back—completely shaken and traumatized. When Jesus finally healed her heart, He said to her, "I took you to Hell because I love you."

She went on to say, "If I had died without God showing that to me, I know I would be there right now!"[15]

This was truly a *rich wound* given out of the lovingkindness of our Father to bring her to repentance and save her from eternal damnation! Be quick to forgive!

Intercession

At times, being engaged in spiritual warfare can have suffering associated with it. It can be similar to the case of Job, where it is not a matter of having an open door to allow the adversary to attack; it's very simply that it's war! And the devil doesn't fight fair! Fear of retaliation is no excuse for shrinking from the battle.

---

15 *Sid Roth's It's Supernatural.* https://www.youtube.com/watch?v=qJP0iJ1Zbjg (accessed 21 June 2019).

Dr. Sam Matthews of Family of Faith Ministries has been charged by God with the intercessory mantle of Rees Howells, a champion intercessor whose prayers with the Bible School of Wales helped to protect the United Kingdom during World War II. The assignments the Lord gives him are not for the faint-hearted. He gets involved in high level spiritual warfare under orders from the Holy Spirit. Many times these prayer battles are for whole nations or whole people groups to see them saved through the Blood of Jesus from the lies that hold them bound.

Sometimes as the battle rages, his wife, Kathy, has come under enemy fire. One such time they were in a battle so intense that Kathy's very life was at stake. The Lord told Dr. Matthews that he would have to prevail in this intercession for his wife to live. In this case, he could not even take her to the doctor, because this sickness was not organic. They would not be able to diagnose it. It was caused by spiritual darkness. It's as though she was being held hostage in a terrible torment of pain while he battled the enemy for her life. At one point, during this four month intercession where she continually lost blood and couldn't eat anything for over fifty days, the pain became so great that she didn't think that she could take it any longer. She cried out to the Lord for His mercy to deliver her from it. In response, she saw a vision of the Lord Jesus on the cross. She saw how terribly He was suffering. He said to her, "I did this for you. Can you do this for Me?" Her heart was melted by His love and great sacrifice and she never complained again of the agony she was in. Although she nearly died, they gained an eternal victory, and she was healed and restored.

One time she was blind for thirteen years while engaged in an intercession against the antichrist spirits[16] of several religions. When a breakthrough came and the victory was

---

16   The god of this world that has blinded the minds of the unbelieving, (2 Corinthians 4:3-4)

won, her eyesight was restored! This intercession is still engaging the powers of evil and deception and gaining victories each day!

As surely as the Lord Jesus "shall see of the travail of his soul, and shall be satisfied,"[17] this couple will be delighted with the eternal outcome of their transitory suffering on earth.

> It will be worth it all when we see Jesus !
> Life's trials will seem so small
> when we see Christ.
> One glimpse of His dear face,
> all sorrow will erase.
> So, bravely run the race
> till we see Christ.[18]

17   Isaiah 53:11a

18   Esther Kerr Rusthoi "When We See Christ" © 1940 New Spring (Admin. by Brentwood-Benson Music Publishing, Inc.) https://songselect.ccli.com/Songs/12004/when-we-see-christ/viewlyrics` (accessed 21 June 2019).

Chapter 13

How?

The basic premise I have tried to share in this book is that no matter how our situations and circumstances appear to our natural reasonings, God has a higher point of view to be able to see "the big picture." He can see the end from the beginning, because He *is* the Beginning and the end. The anguish of suffering is eased by our trust in Him, knowing that His plans are for our good and not for disaster or evil.[1] And if we love Him and are called according to His purpose, we can KNOW that He works all things together for our good.[2]

We don't have to understand. We don't even have to see the "big picture" yet (we will see it one day in wonder and amazement at all the details He put together for our good). As we approach Him in childlike trust, we can leave our circumstances in His hands and simply obey Him when He gives us instructions.

But we are not to remain as babes. Jesus maintained His trust in and obedience to His Father from childhood on, but He GREW UP!

The Apostle Paul explains about this transition:

---

1   Jeremiah 29:11

2   Romans 8:28

When I was a child, I spoke as a child, I understood as a child, I thought as a child: but when I became a man, I put away childish things. For now we see through a glass, darkly; but then face to face: now I know in part; but then shall I know even as also I am known. And now abides faith, hope, love, these three; but the greatest of these is love (1 Corinthians 13:11-13).

As the heavens are high above the earth, so high are the Lord's ways above ours. We cannot continue to reason with the child*ish* reasoning of the carnal nature. Walking in a trusting child*like* relationship with our Father, we don't have to understand the details until He reveals them to us. But we must walk in the revelation He gives us. It's His intent that we become so attuned to the Holy Spirit that we behave like our elder brother, Jesus. The fruit of the Holy Spirit should be manifesting in our lives, and the greatest of these is love—the kind that looks out for the needs of the one loved and provides for them.

Paul puts it this way in Romans chapter five:

Therefore being justified by faith, we have peace with God through our Lord Jesus Christ: By whom also **we have access by faith into this grace** wherein we stand, and rejoice in hope of the glory of God. And not only so, but **we glory in tribulations** also: knowing that **tribulation works patience**; And patience, experience; and experience, hope: And hope makes not ashamed; because **the love of God is shed abroad in our hearts** by the Holy Ghost which is given unto us (Romans 5:1-5).

Do you see the progression? Faith gives us the grace and ability to rejoice in the hope we have of God getting glory in our lives, so we can actually glory in our tribulations because through them we are maturing in patience (that's not something the childish are known for!). This patience gives us experience and experience gives us hope.

I have lived long enough and have walked through enough difficult circumstances to have learned how faithful our Father is. We may not see an answer right away—that's developing patience—but we WILL CERTAINLY see it. It may not be exactly the answer we were expecting, but when it comes, we'll know that God sent it. And we won't be ashamed or disappointed in this hope, because He will surely do what He says He will do, in His way, in His time. He is faithful! Praise and glorify Him for His unfailing love and faithfulness! The outcome will be beyond your imagination!

"My Yoke Is Easy"

After the Board of Directors meeting ended when I officially became the vice president of End-Time Handmaidens and Servants International, I was walking down the sidewalk alone and began pondering the enormity of what just took place. As I was beginning to get overwhelmed, I had a vision. I saw what appeared to be like a large PVC pipe, six inches in diameter, suspended about six inches above my shoulders. It extended about thirty feet in either direction.[3] I understood that it was the yoke of the responsibility of the office of vice president.

Then I saw that it was being held up by an angel on either side of me. They were holding it with their arms down in a relaxed manner nearly by their sides. They were very large!

I understood from what I saw that my job was not to carry the yoke, but to stay under it. I must not run ahead, and I must not lag behind. I didn't have to understand everything that was going along. I just needed to be tuned in, to obey the Holy Spirit and to walk with the

---

3   6 inches = 15.24 cm, 30 feet = 9.14 m

responsibility, but not to be burdened or overwhelmed by it.

When I became the president after our founder's passing, I saw a vision of a much larger, more elaborate "yoke." But I still had the understanding that it was not for me to carry as a "burden," but that I was to be associated with it and not to get out of step with it.

Jesus' Yoke

Jesus promised us that His yoke is easy and His burden is light. Let's look at that passage in context.

In Matthew 11, Jesus encourages the disciples of John the Baptist to return to him and relate what they saw and heard of the blind receiving their sight, the lame walking, the lepers being cleansed, the dead raised, and the Good News preached to the poor. Apparently John was wondering whether Jesus was really the One who was to come or not. He had been imprisoned by this time and was likely experiencing an onslaught from the liar, trying to fill his mind with doubts.

Jesus goes on to talk about John's greatness as the messenger of the Lord, and how he had come as Elijah to proclaim His coming before He came. Then He compares the reception given to both of them. Those who had no heart after God said that John had a devil, for he had come as a Nazarite, neither eating or drinking. Then the same people saw Jesus eating and drinking and called Him gluttonous and a "winebibber." They couldn't recognize truth! They could only repeat accusations.

Then Jesus started to reproach the cities of Chorizin, Bethsaida, and Capernaum for not welcoming Him, saying that it would be more tolerable for Tyre, Sidon, and Sodom in the Judgment. If the works that Jesus was doing in the first three cities had been done in the last three cities, the people would have repented in sackcloth and ashes.

He begins to pray: "I thank You, O Father, Lord of Heaven and Earth, because **You have hidden these things** from the wise and prudent, and have **revealed them unto babes [children** so young that they cannot speak clearly yet]. Amen, Father: **for so it seemed good in Your sight**." Jesus thanked our Father for hiding things from the ones who can reason and for showing them to those who could not!

Apparently He turned to those listening to Him and declared:

> All things are delivered unto Me of My Father: and no man knows the Son, but the Father; neither knows any man the Father, save the Son, and he to whomsoever the Son will reveal Him. Come unto Me, all you that labour and are heavy laden, and I will give you rest. Take My yoke upon you, and learn of Me; for I am meek [gentle, humble] and lowly in heart: and you shall find rest unto your souls. For My yoke is easy [better, ... gracious, kind], and My burden is light [in weight] (Matthew 11:25-30).

Remember that the first thing the Lord said about Himself to Moses on Mount Sinai was that He was merciful like a mother having tender pity toward her infant child. This sounds like the same heart Jesus is describing that He has. As we come to Him like little children that can't even talk properly yet,[4] He will reveal Himself to us more and more. He will lift the heavy burdens of the things we don't understand and give us a break, a rest.

The word used in the Greek for "light" is the same as the "light affliction" the Apostle Paul referred to in

---

4   We really don't have the words to declare His true greatness! That's why we need to speak in tongues!

2 Corinthians 4:17. Let's look at what Paul calls "light affliction":

We are **troubled** on every side, yet not distressed; we are **perplexed**, but not in despair; **Persecuted**, but not forsaken; cast down, but not destroyed; Always bearing about in the body the **dying** of the Lord Jesus, that the life also of Jesus might be made manifest in our body. For we which live are always **delivered unto death** for Jesus' sake, that the life also of Jesus might be made manifest in our mortal flesh. So then death works in us, but life in you. ... For all things are for your sakes, that the abundant grace might through the thanksgiving of many redound to the glory of God. For which cause we faint not; but though our outward man **perish**, yet the inward man is renewed day by day. **For our light affliction, which is but for a moment, works for us a far more exceeding and eternal weight of glory;** *While we look not at the things which are seen, but at the things which are not seen: for the things which are seen are temporal; but the things which are not seen are eternal* (2 Corinthians 4:8-12, 15-18).

Our Father wants to give us eyes to see the eternal— His "big picture," His long-range Plan. When we with childlike trust accept whatever comes our way as being from His hand, it sets us free from fear.

"For you have not received the spirit of bondage again to fear; but you have received the Spirit of adoption, whereby we cry, Abba, Father" (Romans 8:15).

"And deliver them who through fear of death were all their lifetime subject to bondage" (Hebrews 2:15).

God's Time Chart

Of course, if God's ways are so much higher than ours, so is His concept of time. Peter said, "But, beloved, be not ignorant of this one thing, that one day is with the Lord as a thousand years, and a thousand years as one day" (2 Peter 3:8). So let's calculate:

- One day = 1,000 years
- Twelve hours = 500 years
- Six hours = 250 years
- Three hours = 125 years
- One and a half hours = 83.333 years (a lifetime?)
- One hour = 41.667 years
- One minute = 253.68 days (almost 8 1/2 months)
- One second = 4.228 days

We don't think on the same plane as God does—and that's just calculable time by a clock and calendar. That doesn't begin to compare to eternity! When we lose a loved one, we need to consider that it could be only an hour or less, or perhaps just minutes of God's time until we are reunited. When that takes place we will find it to be true! Start thinking about the eternity we have ahead of us!

We have to learn to flow in the Holy Spirit! He is eternal and can tune us to our Father's ways and times.

Dealing with the Past

One of the best things you can do to help free yourself from the slime of shame for personal sin and the generational iniquity that comes down your family line is to take it to the Holy Communion table. The mighty cleansing power of the Blood of Jesus and the wounds He bore for us become tangible with the bread and the cup. We like to use *matzos* for Communion bread because they so clearly show the stripes, the piercings and the bruising that Jesus endured to set us free. You can hold it in your hand and meditate on His finished work. Ask the Holy Spirit to lead you and bring things to mind that need the finished work of Jesus brought to bear over them. The Holy Communion is the key to bringing both the power of Jesus' death and His resurrection into your situation to transform it into a *rich wound*. It is the token of the New Covenant (Jeremiah 31:31-34, Luke 22:20) in the same way that circumcision is the token of the covenant God made with His Chosen People to give them the Promised Land.[5]

Perhaps there is a wound in your life that you need help forgiving. If you have asked Jesus to live in your heart, think about the fact that the Forgiver lives inside of you, and just like He said from the cross, "Father, forgive them, they know not what they do," His Presence in your heart can give you the grace to say the same thing. And when you begin to intercede for the one that hurt you, asking God to forgive that person, the grace to forgive begins to flow into you. Then you receive the elements of the Body and Blood of Jesus and cover that person's sin against you, blotting it out of the record in your soul. That will set you free. Then ask the Lord to convict that person and bring repentance that will also set him/her free. Your forgiveness sets that person free from your judgment and accusation, giving them the opportunity to repent.

You may need to do this daily for some time, until the Lord covers all the territory of wounds in your life. He is gracious to do it a little at a time—perhaps one incident at a time will come to your recall.

---

5   In the New Covenant, God promises to put His law in the inward parts of His Chosen People, and write it in their hearts, that He will be their God, and they will be His People. They will all know Him, for He will forgive their iniquity and remember their sin no more. It's about reconciliation for sin and establishing relationship with the Father. The Gentiles are also grafted into this New Covenant by baptism and receiving Holy Communion as signs of their faith in Jesus' finished work on the cross.

God told the children of Israel when they came into the Promised Land that He wasn't going to drive out all the enemies at once, so the wild animals wouldn't take over when they didn't have a large enough population to occupy the whole Land.[6] It's the same way with growing out of the woundings of the past and iniquities of previous generations. Just deal with the issue the Holy Spirit brings up each day.

Remember the importance of praise and thanksgiving on a daily basis as well. "Giving thanks always for all things unto God and the Father in the name of our Lord Jesus Christ" (Ephesians 5:20). And, "Rejoice evermore. Pray without ceasing. In every thing give thanks: for this is the will of God in Christ Jesus concerning you" (1 Thessalonians 5:16-18).

These are keys to help you be an overcomer and to grow into the maturity of a son of God as Paul mentioned in Romans 8:

> There is therefore now no condemnation to them which are in Christ Jesus, **who walk not after the flesh, but after the Spirit.** ... That the righteousness of the law might be fulfilled in us, **who walk not after the flesh, but after the Spirit.** ... For if you live after the flesh, you shall die: but if you through the Spirit mortify the deeds of the body, you shall live. **For as many as are led by the Spirit of God, they are the sons of God.** For you have not received the spirit of bondage again to fear; but you have received the Spirit of adoption, whereby we cry, Abba, Father. The Spirit itself bears witness with our spirit, that we are the children of God: And if children, then heirs; heirs of God, and **joint-heirs with Christ; if so be that we suffer with Him, that we may be**

---

6   Deuteronomy 7:22

also glorified together. For I reckon that the sufferings of this present time are not worthy to be compared with the glory which shall be revealed in us. For the earnest expectation of the creature waits for the manifestation of the sons of God" (Romans 8:1, 4, 13-19).

"Beloved, **now are we the sons of God**, and it does not yet appear what we shall be: but we know that, when He shall appear, we shall be like Him; for we shall see Him as He is. **And every man that has this hope in him purifies himself, even as He is pure**" (1 John 3:2-3).

Many times the issues of life come in layers, like an onion. Let the Lord deal with each layer, one at a time. He will be faithful to keep at it until the entire job is done.

A Wholesome Tongue

"A wholesome[4832] tongue is a tree of life: but perverseness[5558] therein is a breach[7667] in the spirit" (Proverbs 15:4).

Because "death and life are in the power of the tongue..." (Proverbs 18:21a), the wounds of the tongue are probably the deepest and most devastating wounds possible. This is clearly emotional abuse. When sticks and stones break the bones, the animosity with which they were wielded can cause a wound that goes on after the bones are healed. The saying goes on, "names (or words) will never hurt me," and it couldn't be farther from the truth (unless of course you actually believe it). If the "names" or hurtful words are received in the spirit as true, or as a perception of what the speaker really feels, the results can be devastating. In Luke 6:45 Jesus said that out of the heart the mouth speaks, so you can tell what a person has been meditating about when they blurt something out under pressure.

Strong's Concordance number for the word "perverse" in the scripture at the beginning of this section is H5558 for the Hebrew word "סֶלֶף çeleph, pronounced seh'-lef. distortion, (figuratively) viciousness:— Crookedness, perverseness, crooked dealing.[7] It comes from the word *çalaph* that means to wrench, subvert, overthrow, or pervert."[8]

A tongue that is perverse or distorted comes from a perverse or distorted heart. The truth is that hurt people hurt people! Most abusers were abused as children. The seed of abuse was sown in them and they grew up to manifest the same thing.

The word for "breach" is "Strong's #H7667 רֶבֶשׁ, שֶׁבֶר *sheber, sheh'-ber;* or *shêber*; from H7665; a fracture, figuratively, ruin; specifically, a solution (of a dream):— affliction, breach, breaking, broken(-footed, -handed), bruise, crashing, destruction, hurt, interpretation, vexation."

Do you see how twisted, perverse words bring ruin, affliction, breaking, bruising, destruction to the victim of those words? Then once the tongue lashing is over, does the hurt one mull over the words and imagine what they should have replied? Then vexation sets in and deep damage is done.

In the margin of my *Hebrew Greek Key Study Bible*, the first phrase from the Hebrew could also be rendered: "The healing[4832] of the tongue."

But note that "The healing of the tongue is a tree of life." When your heart gets regenerated, your tongue does too, and it has the capacity to pour out words that will bring healing and life.

7   "çeleph" Strong's #H5558. https://www.blueletterbible.org/lang/lexicon/lexicon.cfm?Strongs=H5558&t=KJV (accessed 22 June 2019).

8   "çalaph" Strong's #H5557 https://www.blueletterbible.org/lang/lexicon/lexicon.cfm?strongs=H5557&t=KJV (accessed 22 June 2019).

"Love Keeps No Record of Wrongs"

The following is from my journal:

"Love keeps no record of wrong.[9] If you want Me not to retain your wrongs, you must not retain in your memory the wrongs of others. If you want Me to cleanse you of your sins and shortcomings by My Blood, then you must use My Blood to wash away your record of the wrongs and offenses of others.

"When you find yourself offended or just annoyed at the actions or words of a sister or brother, ask Me to forgive them and use that grace to forgive them yourself. Apply My Blood to the offense.

"These offenses and petty annoyances are keeping you earthbound and from rising up to the next level that you want to achieve in Me. My Blood is liquid love and it covers the multitude of sins" (1 Peter 4:8).

Let the Light Leak Out

On occasion, the circumstances that take place in a day might make you feel as though you've been slashed to ribbons. On one such day, I wondered how I would be able to go to supper and lead in singing the *Doxology* before our prayer of blessing for the food. I knew that it was essential that I sing from my heart with genuine praise and worship: "Praise God from whom all blessings flow..." As I did, I was delighted to see in the spirit that the places where I felt I had been slashed had become openings for the glory of God that I was feeling on the inside as I praised, to shine through. It was like a torn tent with a lamp inside would leak light through every little shredded place when camping in the darkness.

---

9 1 Corinthians 13:5b

Great Grace

Our founder, Sister Gwen Shaw, told of an incident she observed that has stayed with me for years as a lesson of the grace of God operating in one of His saints who had let Him do His work in her.

Dinner was finished and the ladies were putting the food away in the kitchen. Leona had just put some things in the refrigerator when Valerie, who preferred to go barefoot, came up behind her without her knowledge. Leona moved back and stepped soundly on Valerie's toes.

Shocked at what she had just done, Leona shouted, "Valerie! How many times do I have to tell you not to run around barefooted!"

Valerie soothed, "Oh, Leona, thank you for being so concerned about me!"

Don't be afraid of being wounded. Be quick to forgive. When your cup is tipped, what is going to spill out? Will it be the Love of God that you are meditating on? Or will it be anger or hurt? Let the Blood of the Lamb that was slain wash you and then wash away the sins of others, for *"Whose soever sins you remit, they are remitted unto them; and whose soever sins you retain, they are retained"* (John 20:23). Let's allow the Lord to use us to be carriers of forgiveness and peace.

"Unto Him that loved us, and washed us from our sins in His own blood, ...to Him be glory and dominion for ever and ever. Amen" (Rev.1:5-6).

Hard or Soft?

June Lewis was a brilliant teacher of the Word of God who poured out revelation on the scriptures like refreshing water. She taught in our International School of Ministry for many years.

One of the keys that she taught from her studies of the Old Testament had to do with cleansing of different types of materials. She pointed out that soft things were cleansed with water, and hard things were cleansed with fire.

We always have the opportunity to humble ourselves before the Lord and ask Him to soften our hearts and cleanse ourselves with the washing of the water by the Word.[10] Our Father is so lovingly concerned for us to be cleansed, that if we do not come voluntarily to wash in His Word, He'll send a fire to cleanse us in our hardness of heart.

10   Ephesians 5:26

Chapter 14

Help from Heaven

Burning the Books

As we walk with the Holy Spirit, He will lead us into all truth. That's what Jesus promised in John 16:13. When the Lord allowed Pat Holloran to see "The Presentation" of the angels and babies to each other shortly after birth, He taught him how to deal with the demonic scribe before he could record anything to be used against his granddaughter. This prevents the forever loser from having access to the knowledge of God's plans for her.

Then Pat asked the Lord,

"How can I do this for my children?"

He said, "How about for yourself and your wife as well?"

I said, "That too, Lord. In fact, for all the people that I know. How can I remove this perverse book of remembrance from the library of the enemy?"

And the Lord said, "It is very simple. I will lead you into the enemy places and you will ask Me to take My fire and consume the perverted book of remembrance that has all those things written in it at the time of dedication."

So I said, "Lord, I ask You, take Your fire and go to where the enemy has stored the perverted book of remembrance with my name, my children's names, my son-in-love, my daughter-in-love, and my bride and consume it with Your fire. And then Lord, take the demonic scribe who has a memory of that event and put them under the feet of Jesus Christ." And it happened.[1]

Pat added this prayer to his book:

My God, through the blood of Jesus Christ, I worship you. Jesus Christ, you are my King and my Redeemer, my only way to the Father. My Holy Ghost, you lead me in all truth. You fill my life with victory. Your Word enables me to do the impossible. I am destined right now to have a future and a hope and to fulfill my destiny.

So I ask You, Holy Ghost, to pray for me now with groanings that cannot be uttered, and I ask You, my Lord, to petition for myself, my family, my friends, my relatives, loved ones, relationships, and my covenants, to the Father of the heavens and that you would prepare the righteous fire now to consume all perverted books of remembrance that have come from the time when I was a brand new baby and when my friends and family and those I know and care about were brand new babies, my children and my grandchildren as well. I ask You, my God, to take Your fire and go to the enemy's library and for You to battle in the heavens, for it is written, even the heavens are the Lord's.

And I ask You to take Your holy fire and to consume these books now. Now burn this evil up and any that would remain; place them immediately

1   Holloran, Pat, *Foundations of the Supernatural Lifestyle* (Palm Harbor: Harvest House International Ministries, 2011), 78.

under the feet of Jesus Christ, for it is written, whom the Son sets free is free indeed. And now, my Lord, I speak into the dimensions and the heavenly places that all demonic scribes that wrote into these perverted books shall now be placed without delay under the feet of Jesus Christ.

And as You do this, I ask that You would make new my mantles, the gifts, and the callings of You, my God, that are in my life, Your ministry that is in my life, and I ask you to remove all spirits of illegitimacy, abandonment, divorce, and betrayal, and put all this evil immediately under the feet of Jesus Christ.

And now, Holy Ghost, fill me up, fill those that I have prayed and petitioned for, and that You, Holy Ghost of promise, would seal us up now in the name of Jesus Christ. And it is written, "Wisdom, you are my sister; understanding, I call you my intimate friend." It is also written, "those who sow in tears will reap in joy," so be it now. I declare, it is written, "for I know the plans I have for you, says the Lord, a future and a hope." Not sickness, not pain, not disease, not poverty, not impoverishment, all that evil must get now get under the feet of Jesus Christ.

Now, my Lord, I ask for brand new armor, every piece, and especially help me to pick up the shield of faith. I want Your might, my Lord. I will change this region, I will change the land I am on and will be on. I will be a vessel that is more than a conqueror. I am a saint of Bethel of heaven on earth. I see what my King does in heaven, so be it.

And my Lord, right now I ask in Jesus Christ's name that You would activate that part of the brain that causes people to see the supernatural world.

That where they are in their discernment at its highest will be their Stage One. And then my King of kings, I ask You to petition the Father to have the Holy Ghost raise that discernment gifting up half a point every week until it rises to a ten. And Lord, do not let any of this overtake the people.

And now I ask You to activate it, that these all would be Your people and that they would be Your messengers in the house, in the job, and they would be vessels of honor and grace, and that they would support their leaders and that their leaders would step into mantles of fathering. And I ask that in this land every leader will step into the third great awakening for our land.

Then Pat goes on to pray this prayer for those who were reading his book:

The people who are reading this book, Lord, I commission them into Your hands as they honor authority, as they submit to the authority of the vessels that are put by You on the land to be in that position. And I ask for the fear of the Lord to consume everyone. Holy Ghost, give everybody around me who follows Jesus Christ, Your anointing. Give them the fear of the Lord and delight in the Lord and the joy of the Lord. Give them strength tactics to do their destiny. Bless their coming in and their going out.

When they wake up, give them prophetic dreams that they would remember and then the interpretation and understanding. I ask, as we close this time, that you will remove them and their angels out of the firing line and that there will be no retaliation as you put a hedge of protection in front and behind them. Now raise up these people and their families, to hear your voice so clearly that they will be sons and daughters of thunder. I submit it to you in the name of Jesus Christ. Amen.[2]

More of Annie's Visions

Lights Over Shadows

As the Lord took me into the Spirit, He said, "Fear not. I have prepared you for the battle," adding that the battles that He prepared for His people are not for the purpose of defeat nor for their wounding, but rather they were to cause them to draw near unto Him.

Then taking me into His lovely presence in that high place where He ever dwells in the glory of His cloud of fire, He told me to look. As I looked I saw far below the forces of the enemy like frightening shadows of darkness like immense mountains. Furthermore they were attacking His own ones whom I saw like lovely lights filled with glorious life. These shadows were battling against those lights trying to cover them, put them out and destroy them in their fury. Then suddenly those living lights who loved Him and were loved by Him rose up in anger and fury and great strength against those horrible shadows. As they stamped upon them flattening them under their feet they were drawing nearer unto Him. These battles and victories were effectively lifting them nearer unto Jesus.

"When I permit the enemy to attack my own loved ones," He said to me," I never take any risks of any kind at any time. For the enemy can never win the battle against them."[3]

---

2   Ibid. 82-85

3   Miller, R. Edward. *I Looked and I Saw Mysteries.* https://revivalcarriers.org/free-downloadable-ebooks-by-r-edward-miller/free-ebook-i-saw-mysteries/ (accessed 10 June 2019).

The Despised Fountain

Taking me away into the spirit and gently receiving me unto Himself, He spoke away all my fears, causing His love to wash over me in great billows of gentle sweetness. "What I have given you none can ever take away, for I have given it to you and I am with you," He said.

When He bade me look I saw a large group of people disconsolate and sorrowful. Upon seeing the sorrow and troubled state of these people I felt a great sadness for I saw that they were His people. When He spoke He told me not to be sad for them, explaining that they were in great sorrow, not because He had left them, but because they desired to be in that condition. They had despised, ridiculed and forsaken that which He had given them, not ever desiring to receive it. Therefore they were disconsolate.

Then I saw as it were a beautiful fountain filled with sparkling waters of life, light and blessing. Yet His own ones were running about all disoriented, searching everywhere for water save in the fountain which He had prepared for them. In their desperate hunt for water they avoided and even refused to draw near unto the place of the fountain.

Although they cried out desperately unto Him and repented, yet He did not answer them or help them at all. Nevertheless, I saw that He was with them. All the while He was carefully watching them: and continually offering unto them the waters of the fountain.

"I do not help them," He said, "because I have already told them what to do. They already know.

Eventually they shall become so desperate that they shall surrender and draw near to partake of the water of the fountain that I have already given them."[4]

The Beautiful Stones

As I was in a hotel room in a neighboring city, I wondered much if I would be able to enter into His presence in such a place and atmosphere. Soon I found it was no different there than being in my own room. After a time of prayer, He came and took me away unto Himself, filling the deep desires of my heart by flooding me with the glories of His amazing love. And, as ever, He swept away all my fears.

After saying, "My fires are not in vain; they burn in order to make my own a very part of me," He showed me the living stones which were broken and appeared most ordinary. Then His fires began to burn upon all of them, burning and wounding certain parts of each one. Each time this fire burned it left something beautiful within these stones. Again and again it came, and each time it left them more beautiful. This process continued until they became no longer merely stones, but had been transformed into reigning fires.

He told me that His fires were not sent in jest, ridicule or capriciousness. Everything that causes pain and comes from His hand is actually wonderful and desirable over there. Each pain is a part of the process of transforming the living stones into reigning fires. The reigning fires became so, not because they were specifically chosen to be, but because they had permitted all His fires to do

4   Ibid.

their work in them. This process had completely transformed them into the reigning fires who ever reign with Him in His Cloud in the highest heavens and who are exactly like Him.

Just as His wounds were so changed and made more beautiful according to each sphere in which He had manifested Himself, in the same manner all the woundings, pains and fires through which He permits His own to pass causes them to become progressively more beautiful until they are literally adorned by wondrous jewels which before were but scars.

As He explained this to me I felt so identified in the work the fires were doing. At last I could understand the reasons for the processes in my own life which heretofore had given me so much pain and insecurity.[5]

His Chariot

Today I was terribly nervous because I was scheduled to take the whole evening chapel service and I was greatly afraid. In prayer I was given to intercede for the people in strong crying. After a while He took me away unto Himself and showed me how He sent forth a special force—as it were a chariot—to bring man unto Himself. This force He used to bring all of His own ever nearer and closer to Himself. This chariot was not made of fire but of special forces which were tribulations, trials, pains and sufferings.

The Lord, Himself, was occupied with the placing or withdrawing of these forces and His purpose was to bring His own unto Himself in order that He might reveal Himself and allow His

---

5   Ibid.

word concerning Himself and His being to shine forth to them. These forces came into operation by His word alone. He did not allow any other, not even the people themselves, this responsibility. He alone ordained and sent forth these forces which like homing chariots would ever draw and bring His own ones ever nearer unto Himself.

Nor would He permit anyone else to withdraw these forces until they had done their good work. Before His set time no one was allowed to touch them for they must accomplish that for which they were sent forth and must not cease until the chariot returned to His very door. Whether it be pain or sufferings, problems or dark clouds, trials or persecutions or any other force of tribulation, all were sent forth from Him. And He was quite ready and willing to send forth even more, and one after another, in order to be certain that His people should reach Him.

As they reached Him they must then be separated from that force and trial. They must no longer abide in His chariot but alight from it and come into His house, as it were. Although He had no pleasure in sending forth these forces, He took great pleasure in bringing His own ones unto Himself.

Nevertheless, He did not desire them to stop in the way and begin to behold the chariot. They must not look at the pressures He was using, for to do so resulted in a delaying of the journey. These forces would do their work effectively and certainly, but His people must keep on traveling forward, ever keeping their eyes upon Him and upon their destination and not on the forces he was using.

The Lord concerned Himself with the withdrawing of these forces at the right moment when the chariot of the forces of tribulation would be dismissed having fulfilled its task and having brought His own to the place He desired.[6]

Paths of Power

Again He showed me the works of His love among His own ones. Although He reigns in the high glory of His fiery reigning Cloud far beyond all things in the high and holy majesty of His person, at the same time, He is somehow able to be in the midst of His own people here upon the earth. Even though they cannot see Him, nevertheless, He is here in their midst and He never leaves them.

The Lord was marking out pathways for His own: pathways of power and love filled with shining glory and wondrous light and, at the same time, pathways of tribulations and trials that would bring pain and sufferings as well. His own ones who chose to walk His marked paths would feel the pain and suffer the reproaches of Christ because they had accepted His paths and were walking in them.

Another people who were offered these same paths refused them, for they would not willingly accept anything that would bring them pain or suffering. These did not want to suffer these things for Him nor to fulfill His will for them and to them were given other pathways in which to walk. Although I couldn't see what kind of paths they were, I realized that they had thereby lost all

---

6   Miller, R. Edward. *I Looked & I Saw The Heavens Opened.* https://revivalcarriers. org/free-downloadable-ebooks-by-r-edward-miller/free-ebook-i-saw-heavens-opened/ 44-45

opportunity to taking those first paths that He had marked out for them.

Those who had accepted those paths which were marked out by the Master for them were conducted directly through those paths unto Jesus, Himself, being thereby brought into a very glorious and large manifestation of Him. Thus were they made like unto Him.[7]

The Power of Self-Knowledge

In prayer today the Lord showed me a people on the earth below upon whom He was pouring out a certain power that came forth from Him with great light. This power was most penetrating and would burrow its way through, as it were, into the innermost parts like some type of perforating machine. Coming forth in great might, it brought with it the power of a strong light force.

This brilliant light-power was the power of self-knowledge or the ability to know and perceive one's own inner self—an inner revelation of light and truth. This power was cold, penetrating and wounding and would pierce through defenses and through flesh into the interior. Although it was a wounding, piercing force, yet withal it was not destructive; it was painful and not the most welcome blessing sent forth from God. But still it was sent forth from God and came as a blessing to these people. It had the power to illuminate the inner recesses of the heart and reveal the things hidden therein in the spirit of truth, discovering all hidden deceits and bringing them forth unto the light.

---

7   Ibid. 59.

This power was accompanied by another power, the power of wisdom. This second power was neither cold nor wounding; rather, it was warm and filled with tender love. The light that accompanied this power of wisdom was not severe but rather was a healing light which brought healing to all the wounds caused by the penetrating, piercing power of self-knowledge. I saw that the power of wisdom and the healing light worked together to bring forth enlightened understanding and dissolve confusions and deceits. Not only did they bring forth healing and understanding but, at the same time, they also worked a wonderful transformation in the inner being. This was not an instantaneous operation but was prolonged and ever increased in its perfections, working through a process and during a period of time. This process was universal to all of those to whom He sent it and it was continuous and not an intermittent process.

I also understood that the majority of the people rejected the cold, penetrating power of self-knowledge. They were afraid of its operation and of the pain that came with it. Therefore, they were incapacitated or unable to receive the accompanying power of wisdom and of healing light because they could only receive the power of wisdom as they allowed the power of self-knowledge to first do its needed work.

The act of rejecting the power of self-knowledge sent forth from God closed the understanding and it remained dark, enclosed within its own darkness of deceit. This rejection also closed the people to the second healing, enlightening power of wisdom. It could not find entrance neither could it function in them.[8]

---

8   Ibid. 61-61.

Challenges

In the realms of light the Lord showed me the entrances into progressive levels of light. Before each level, a divine challenge faced His own ones which was not defined to me but was, nevertheless, very real and obvious.

These challenges had the appearance of negative values, as if they would be harmful to one if accepted; nevertheless, the truth was that each challenge of the Lord—if accepted—would lead His own ones on into a higher level of light. To reject a challenge from the Lord caused one to lose the light which it was meant to bring. These challenges, which were many, were progressive.

Later He told me that the stream of ministry would increase each time it flowed forth, and in this way would become progressively more useful.[9]

Pathways with Pain

His light, radiant in revelation, shone into my spirit as the Lord showed me a pathway in which there was a "wounding" of all those who entered. This wounding caused a pain that was positive and good, and not at all destructive; nor was it the working of the powers of darkness. For a long time, this wounding caused pain to those who walked in this pathway; in fact, the pain lasted until they arrived at the end preset by the Lord Himself.

Then He showed me another pathway which was also a pathway of wounding and pain. In the first pathway there had been one original wounding

---

9   Ibid. 86.

which had caused pain throughout the whole length of its course and never healed; in contrast, this second pathway was filled with wounding one after the other. There was a wounding, and then a self-healing began immediately which continued on until the wound had quickly healed. Being completely restored, it now caused no more pain. Then suddenly the traveler in that second pathway received yet another wounding from God. The healing processes again began quickly, and brought healing and cessation of pain. This wounding and self-healing process continued right on during the full length of the entire course.

Then the Lord showed me that it was His own ones—the sons of light—who were walking in one or the other of these two pathways. Those who walked in the second pathway, which was so full of woundings, discovered that it was by far the more valuable way. The weight of glory in the second path far superseded that in the first pathway which had but one initial wounding and pain throughout its course, without any self-healing processes.

He continued to speak to me concerning His pathways. Before the sons of light stood what appeared to be sections. In each section there were obstacles and obstructions which had been placed there as prerequisites for the fulfilling of that section. If that son did not overcome the obstacles in that next section, he could no longer remain there, but had to return and remain in the previous section whose obstacles he had already overcome.[10]

10 Ibid. 87. I highly recommend the books of Annie's visions. There is so much more than we have quoted. See https://revivalcarriers.org/free-downloadable-ebooks-by-r-edward-miller/

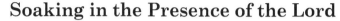

Soaking in the Presence of the Lord

Soaking in the Presence of the Lord begins with becoming aware of your eternal Father who is there all the time. His Spirit, His Presence, is like oxygen—you can't sense it with your five natural senses, but it's all around you, and you can't live without it. According to Jeremiah 23:23-24, God's Presence is everywhere; He fills Heaven and Earth. But all too often you are unaware of His Presence because you are not fully living and walking in the Spirit, which is your inheritance. Unhurriedly staying for a while in His Presence changes you in the same way that fabric soaking in dye changes its appearance, or a cucumber soaking in brine changes its flavor. When saturation occurs, you will never be the same. You are eternally transformed.

When you soak in His Presence, you become aware of His attributes. All of the fruit of the Holy Spirit (love, joy, peace, patience toward others, kindness, goodness, faithfulness, gentleness, and self-control) become accessible to you, but the greatest of these is love. This kind of love is inexpressible, no mere words can contain it. It gives you everything you need and crave in your innermost being. Then the healing begins. Things you couldn't put right for yourself become adjusted as His manifestation fills your empty places and reveals to you His passion for your soul.

As God's peace envelops you, all the looming possibilities suggested or threatened by the darkness collapse as the light of the Lord's countenance shines on you. You are set free from bondage to fear, and faith takes its place. Deep trust comes and grows deeper the longer you remain in that place.

Staying in the awareness of His Presence inspires you to grow up in Him. His Presence pours out the grace to overcome your fleshly immaturity—the grace to become all that He made you to be—the grace to walk as a mature son of your Father. It's like entering into the family business as a partner, doing business on your Father's behalf with His guidance and blessing.

Perhaps you will hear a message from His heart in your spirit: words of comfort, instruction or direction. Or maybe it will be an impression that comes without words; you will have an idea, perhaps a concept, a revelation that can close a door from the past and open a new one for your future. Hope ignites in your soul. The need you couldn't put into words is met and your faith steps up to accept that God is all you need.

In Him is life—it exudes from Him and penetrates your soul, freeing you from the wages of sin. Truth pours out from Him and destroys lies. Your heart becomes assured and at rest in this confidence: that because He is all His Word says He is, you are also all He says you are. As you rest in His Presence, He resets you, from glory to glory.

Sometimes the Holy Spirit points out a place in your life where your old nature that was crucified with Christ is still trying to operate. He ministers an upgrade into that area, helping you to possess a share of the divine nature because He lives within you, and the old ways wither out of existence. As God cleanses your imagination, your mind is renewed and you begin to grow in the prophetic.

Being in the Presence of God in the present opens a window into eternity. You may be caught away to view the glories of your eternal home. You could have visions of biblical events in the past, or the future.

In His Presence comes the revelation of God's call on your life. You begin to feel His heart for the lost as His love compels you to share your life in Him with your neighbor or a stranger. Perhaps He will put a nation or people group on your heart, and intercession for His outpouring will come from deep within you, making a difference in the spirit realm over those people. Perhaps He will lead you to go somewhere in His service, and the grace that comes from His Presence will cause joyful obedience to well up inside you.

The Holy Spirit fills and refills you, each time transforming your walk and relationship with Him, as you practice His Presence.

Grace and peace be multiplied to you from God your Father, and from the Lord Jesus Christ as you make His Presence a priority in your life.

When He Has Tried Me

by Gwen R. Shaw / Sharon Buss

Chorus
When He has tried me, I'll come forth as gold;
The fires of affliction will not harm my soul;
I know that God loves me. My life has a goal;
And when He has tried me, I'll come forth as gold.

Verse 1
When through fiery trials God calls me to go,
I won't be discouraged, Nor fear for my soul;
Jesus is coming, His pure bride to claim,
Washed in His blood and tried by the flame.

Verse 2
My great trial of faith is more precious than gold.
I've forsaken earth's treasures for His wealth untold;
Glory and honours are waiting for me,
When up in Heav'n His face I shall see.

Chapter 15

Points to Ponder

Neither time nor space allow the development of all the little notes I have made through the years on this subject. So, rather than just leave them out, I felt to include them as thoughts for your meditation. The same Holy Spirit Who breathed them into me will give you a "download" from the heart of our Father.

- Steel is forged in fire for strength.

- Glass is tempered in fire for safety.

- Costly stones come from fire. God uses heat or heat and pressure in the formation of many gemstones. That will preach!

- Wishful thinking says, "everything is going to be good!" The truth is it is going to be good if you love the Lord and are called according to His purpose. But that doesn't mean that everything will be good along the way. We will have lots of opportunities to encounter bad events. But how we approach them will have a great deal to do with how we come out of them.

- John Arnott: "God offends our mind to show us what is in our hearts."

- Give it to God and see what He will do with it.

- Treading grapes yields whatever is in them—sweetness in the ripe, sourness or bitterness from those that haven't spent enough time in the sun or drawn from the dung that has been given to them for fertilizer.

- Perhaps our situation may seem like "dung" but we have to look for how that will work as fertilizer to help us grow strong and bear fruit.

- The vines must "suffer," that is, grow under harsh conditions, in order to produce the sweetest fruit and therefore the sweetest wine.

- Olives have to be crushed over and over to get out the oil for anointing, for food, and for light.

- "4 tons of roses = 1 600 000 rose blossoms = 1 kg of rose oil. No wonder rose oil is one of the most expensive essences."[1]

- Grain must be ground into flour to feed the hungry (unless you sprout it first, then you mash it).

- The greater the wounds, the more glorious the reward.

- "To glorify" is the Greek word, "*DOXAZO* (G1390); From *DOXA* (G1391), glory, to glorify, to recognize, honor, praise… To bring honor,… Make glorious… in the writings of John, the *DOXA* of God is the revelation and manifestation of all that He has and is. It is His revelation in which He manifests all the goodness that He is (John 12:28). Since Christ made this manifest, He is said to glorify the father…; or the father is glorified in Him…. When Christ is said to be glorified, it means simply

---

1   https://boisdejasmin.com/2014/02/rose-harvest-in-turkey.html (accessed 24 June 2019).

that His innate glory is brought to light, made manifest....[2]

- Change the shape of head—renewal of the mind—in preparation for entering a whole new environment of love and growth.

- In the womb all is happy until growth confines. As we grow up in God, sooner or later we have to come out into our destiny.

- Outside the body you are more alive than in it. Sin makes our earthly life constantly subject to death. It's the location where Satan operates with his cohorts to kill, steal, and destroy.

- Give no place to the devil. He's the forever loser!

- The Shepherd has to break the leg of a naughty, rebellious lamb to preserve its life. Then he carries it on His shoulders until it's well, feeding it by hand. From that time, the lamb is inseparable from the Shepherd because of the relationship of love that developed when it was broken.

- Jesus was not afraid of dying—He became sin for us. He took on a "mantle" of sin.

- A newborn baby with congenital heart defects or other life-threatening conditions may have to go through multiple surgeries in order to survive. These are wounds for the purpose of healing in order to have destiny.

- Grow up! Let petty annoyances go! "Fools show their annoyance at once, but the prudent overlook an insult" (Proverbs 12:16 NIV).

---

2 *"Doxazo."* Strong's G1390 definition from "Lexical Aids to the New Testament" by Spiros Zodhiates, *Hebrew Greek Key Study Bible,* (c) 1984 and 1991 Spiros Zodhiates and AMG International, Inc. Chattanooga, TN.

Faithful Are the Wounds of a Friend

- "Faithful are the wounds of a friend; but the kisses of an enemy are deceitful" (Proverbs 27:6). Who speaks into your life? Can they be honest without you getting offended?

- You can't change the circumstances, but you can change your reaction. Agree with your adversary (Matthew 5:25). There is probably some truth to the accusations of the accuser of the brethren. Be brutally honest. Let the plumb line of the Word of God change you.

- Loved ones have the greatest power to hurt us.

- To your own self be true. Don't lie to yourself!

- Bodybuilders understand the principle of "no pain, no gain."

- When we all come into the maturity of sons of God, we will not necessarily be alike. But we will have the same uniform, just like an army. We will be clothed in Christ, and we will hear and obey the Holy Spirit.

Covenant Scars

- When you have "cut covenant" (that is make a blood covenant) with someone, when you hold up your hand before an enemy and show your scar, you are demonstrating that you have someone you are in covenant with who will come to your aid and make war with your enemies.

"Just forgive."

- It was time to start a meeting. I knew I couldn't lead worship with these feelings in my heart toward someone who had hurt me. I was searching my heart for an answer to overcome. Then I heard the Holy Spirit whisper to me, "Just forgive her." What a revelation! In a flash I was free, and the anointing flowed in the worship service.

God Turns Bad Situations into Good

• Joshua and the princes of Israel were deceived into making a covenant with the Gibeonites, a people group who lived in Canaan. So God made provision for them to be servants to cut wood and draw water for the House of God. Then, when the other local kings learned that they had made peace with Israel, they attacked the Gibeonites who called for Joshua to come and rescue them. It was during this battle that Joshua called for the sun and moon to stand still. God responded to give a miracle of the *cosmos* to defend an oath that never should have happened!

• Rahab **the harlot** hid the two spies that Joshua had sent to check out Jericho before the children of Israel entered the Promised Land. She and her family were spared when Jericho fell and she married one of the spies. She is mentioned in the genealogy of Jesus.

• A famine in Bethlehem made Elimelech and Naomi take their two sons to Moab to live. The sons married Moabite women, then all the men of the family died. One of the women, Ruth, returned to Judah with Naomi, married Boaz, and became the great-grandmother of King David. She is mentioned in the genealogy of Jesus.

• King David had an adulterous affair with Bathsheba, and had her husband, Uriah, killed to try and hide her pregnancy (her baby died). Her grandfather,

Ahithophel (David's wisest counsellor), was apparently so angry with David that he followed David's son Absalom who tried to depose David. Ahithophel and Absalom both died and David continued to be king. David appointed Bathsheba's second son, Solomon, to be his successor to the throne. The DNA for wisdom came through from his grandfather, and Solomon was the wisest man who ever lived. Bathsheba was also mentioned in Jesus' genealogy.

Don't Listen to the accuser

Many years ago, I would be up late at night after the rest of the household was asleep. As I was getting ready for bed, I would start to get these harassing thoughts, accusing Sister Gwen to me. Being tired, I began to meditate on them and I'd get angry and upset at her . The next day, she would greet me lovingly, and I'd wonder if what I had thought the night before might not be true.

Then sure enough, that night I'd have the same thing happen. I don't know how long it took me to wake up to the fact that I was hosting the accuser of the brethren. The night I realized it, I said, "Shut up, devil, I'm too tired for this." At which point I put it out of my mind. It returned a few times, but I had learned how to deal with it. I didn't take very many times of rebuking it before it stopped completely.

Don't Allow Your Wounds to Fester

Many years ago, the Lord allowed me to experience some pain that taught me a great lesson.

My husband, Philip, and I were attending a camp. The dormitory room we were given had the most efficiently laid out tiny bathroom I have ever been in. Every inch was utilized.

We were getting ready for one of the meetings and Philip had plugged in a clothes steamer in the bathroom, next to the sink. At some point, while he was standing at the sink, I also needed a little bit of water for something, so I stepped in next to him. I had seen the steamer earlier. I knew it was there. But in that moment, in my hurry, I forgot that hazard. And in a moment, I had burned my leg! Thankfully, we had some aloe vera gel with us. I slathered the wound, and the pain stopped immediately. I went on about getting ready for the day and took a shower. It didn't dawn on me that I showered off the aloe vera gel. Some hours later while dancing in the praise and worship service, I noticed that my skirt was irritating my leg. I stopped to look, and was horrified to discover that the burn had blistered, broken and festered in those few hours. And it took a long time to heal.

I went to the Lord about it later asking why He allowed it to happen. I was given to understand that this would be a sermon illustration for me. It is what happens when we are wounded in our souls. If we will immediately put the Blood of Jesus Christ on the wound, it will immediately lose its pain. But we have to maintain that position. We have to keep it covered under the Blood. If we allow the accuser to remind us of the wounding (that is, replaying the memory of the incident and/or failing to forgive the wounder), the wound will fester and take a long time to heal.

Heavenly Reality

Seeing then that we have a great high priest, that is passed into the heavens, Jesus the Son of God, let us hold fast our profession. For we have not a high priest which cannot be touched with the feeling of our infirmities; but was in all points tempted like as we are, yet without sin. Let us therefore come boldly unto the throne of grace, that we may obtain mercy, and find grace to help in time of need (Hebrews 4:14-16).

He went through all the intense temptation that we have gone through. More work was done in that time to repair the world than to tear it down and build it again.

Wholeness

"And the very God of peace **sanctify**[37] you **wholly**;[3651] and I pray God your **whole**[3648] spirit and soul and body be preserved **blameless** unto the coming of our Lord Jesus Christ. **Faithful is He that calls you, who also will do it**" (1 Thessalonians 5:23-24).

Strong's #G37 *hagiázō*, (hag-ee-ad'-zo); from G40; to make holy, i.e. (ceremonially) purify or consecrate; (mentally) to venerate:—hallow, be holy, sanctify.

Outline of Biblical Usage:

I. to render or acknowledge, or to be venerable or hallow

II. to separate from profane things and dedicate to God

    A.   consecrate things to God

    B.   dedicate people to God

III.   to purify

    A. to cleanse externally

    B. to purify by expiation: free from the guilt of sin

    C. to purify internally by renewing of the soul[3]

Strong's #G3651 *holoteles*, hol-ot-el-ace'; from G3650 and G5056; complete to the end, i.e. absolutely perfect:— wholly.

---

3   "*hagiázō*" https://www.blueletterbible.org/lang/lexicon/lexicon.cfm?Strongs=G37&t=KJV (accessed 24 June 2019).

Outline of Biblical Usage:

I. perfect, complete in all respects[4]

Strong's #G3648 *holóklēros*, hol'-ok'-lay-ros; from G3650 and G2819; complete in every part, i.e. perfectly sound (in body):—entire, whole.[5]

> *holóklēros*; From *hólos* (350), all, the whole, and *klēros* (2819), a part, share. Whole, having all its parts, sound, perfect. That which retains all which was allotted to it at the first, wanting nothing for its completeness; bodily, mental and moral entireness. It expresses the perfection of man before the Fall (1 Thess. 5:23, James 1:4).... **The *holóklēros* is one who has preserved, or who, having once lost has now regained his completeness.** In the *holóklēros*, No grace which ought to be in a Christian... is deficient.[6]

Paul's prayer for us is straight from the heart of God, showing His intention for us as we grow up in Him. His greatest joy is for us to give ourselves completely to Him so that He can purify us entirely according to the price that was paid by Jesus. Then, His intent is to restore to us what He put in us for a destiny, before we were ever marred by sin, so that nothing is broken or missing. That sounds like the definition of *shalom*.

"In the Bible, the word *shalom* is most commonly used to refer to a state of affairs, one of well-being, tranquility, prosperity, and security, circumstances unblemished by

---

4 *"Holoteles"* https://www.blueletterbible.org/lang/lexicon/lexicon. cfm?Strongs=G3651&t=KJV (accessed 24 June 2019).

5 *"Holóklēros."* https://www.blueletterbible.org/lang/lexicon/lexicon. cfm?Strongs=G3648&t=KJV (accessed 24 June 2019).

6 *"Holóklēros."* Strong's G3648 definition from "Lexical Aids to the New Testament" by Spiros Zodhiates, *Hebrew Greek Key Study Bible,* (c) 1984 and 1991 Spiros Zodhiates and AMG International, Inc. Chattanooga, TN

any sort of defect. Shalom is a blessing, a manifestation of divine grace."[7]

"Now unto him that is able to keep you from falling, and to present you faultless before the presence of His glory with exceeding joy, To the only wise God our Saviour, be glory and majesty, dominion and power, both now and ever. Amen" (Jude 1:24-25).

7   https://www.myjewishlearning.com/article/shalom/ (accessed 24 June 2019).

Appendix

Scriptures

Psalm 51:17: The fountain of your pleasure is found in the sacrifice of my shattered heart before you. You will not despise my tenderness as I humbly bow down at your feet (TPT).

Psalm 119:165: Great peace have they which love thy law: and nothing shall offend them.

Isaiah 43:1-7, 10-11, 18-21, 25: But now thus says the LORD that created you, O Jacob, and He that formed you, O Israel, Fear not: for I have redeemed you, I have called you by your name; you are Mine. When you pass through the waters, I will be with you; and through the rivers, they shall not overflow you: when you walk through the fire, you shall not be burned; neither shall the flame kindle upon you. For I am the LORD your God, the Holy One of Israel, your Saviour: I gave Egypt for your ransom, Ethiopia and Seba for you. Since you were precious in My sight, you have been honourable, and I have loved you: therefore will I give men for you, and people for your life. Fear not: for I am with you: I will bring your seed from the east, and gather you from the west; I will say to the north, Give up; and to the south, Keep not back: bring My sons from far, and My daughters from the ends of the earth; Even every one that is called by My name:

for I have created him for My glory, I have formed him; yea, I have made him. ... You are My witnesses, says the LORD, and My servant whom I have chosen: that you may know and believe Me, and understand that I am He: before Me there was no God formed, neither shall there be after Me. I, even I, am the LORD; and beside Me there is no saviour.... Remember not the former things, neither consider the things of old. Behold, I will do a new thing; now it shall spring forth; shall you not know it? I will even make a way in the wilderness, and rivers in the desert. The beast of the field shall honour Me, the dragons and the owls: because I give waters in the wilderness, and rivers in the desert, to give drink to My people, My chosen. This people have I formed for Myself; they shall shew forth My praise.... I, even I, am He that blots out your transgressions for My own sake, and will not remember your sins.

Isaiah 55:11: For as the rain comes down, and the snow from heaven, and returns not thither, but waters the earth, and makes it bring forth and bud, that it may give seed to the sower, and bread to the eater: So shall My word be that goes forth out of My mouth: it shall not return unto Me void, but it shall accomplish that which I please, and it shall prosper in the thing whereto I sent it.

Matthew 6:33: But seek (aim at and strive after) first of all His kingdom and His righteousness (His way of doing and being right), and then all these things taken together will be given you besides (AMPC).

Romans 8:18: For I reckon that the sufferings of this present time are not worthy to be compared with the glory which shall be revealed in us.

1 Corinthians 3:15: If any man's work shall be burned, he shall suffer loss: but he himself shall be saved; yet so as by fire.

2 Corinthians 1:5-7: For as the sufferings of Christ abound in us, so our consolation also abounds by Christ. And whether we be afflicted, it is for your consolation and salvation, which is effectual in the enduring of the same sufferings which we also suffer: or whether we be comforted, it is for your consolation and salvation. And our hope of you is steadfast, knowing, that as you are partakers of the sufferings, so shall you be also of the consolation.

2 Corinthians 5:21: For He has made Him to be sin for us, who knew no sin; that we might be made the righteousness of God in Him.

Ephesians 5:2: And walk in love, as Christ also has loved us, and has given himself for us an offering and a sacrifice to God for a sweet smelling savour.

Philippians 3:8: Yes, furthermore, I count everything as loss compared to the possession of the priceless privilege (the overwhelming preciousness, the surpassing worth, and supreme advantage) of knowing Christ Jesus my Lord and of progressively becoming more deeply and intimately acquainted with Him [of perceiving and recognizing and understanding Him more fully and clearly]. For His sake I have lost everything and consider it all to be mere rubbish (refuse, dregs), in order that I may win (gain) Christ (the Anointed One) (AMPC).

Philippians 3:10: That I may know Him, and the power of His resurrection, and the fellowship of His sufferings, being made conformable unto His death;

Colossians 1:24: Who now rejoice in my sufferings for you, and fill up that which is behind of the afflictions of Christ in my flesh for His body's sake, which is the church:

Colossians 3:1-3: If then you have been raised with Christ [to a new life, thus sharing His resurrection from

189

the dead], aim at and seek the [rich, eternal treasures] that are above, where Christ is, seated at the right hand of God. And set your minds and keep them set on what is above (the higher things), not on the things that are on the earth. For [as far as this world is concerned] you have died, and your [new, real] life is hidden with Christ in God.

Colossians 3:12-15: Clothe yourselves therefore, as God's own chosen ones (His own picked representatives), [who are] purified and holy and well-beloved [by God Himself, by putting on behavior marked by] tenderhearted pity and mercy, kind feeling, a lowly opinion of yourselves, gentle ways, [and] patience [which is tireless and long-suffering, and has the power to endure whatever comes, with good temper]. Be gentle and forbearing with one another and, if one has a difference (a grievance or complaint) against another, readily pardoning each other; even as the Lord has [freely] forgiven you, so must you also [forgive]. And above all these [put on] love and enfold yourselves with the bond of perfectness [which binds everything together completely in ideal harmony]. And let the peace (soul harmony which comes) from Christ rule (act as umpire continually) in your hearts [deciding and settling with finality all questions that arise in your minds, in that peaceful state] to which as [members of Christ's] one body you were also called [to live]. And be thankful (appreciative), [giving praise to God always]. (AMPC)

Hebrews 2:10: For it became Him, for whom are all things, and by whom are all things, in bringing many sons unto glory, to make the captain of their salvation perfect through sufferings.

Hebrews 10:34: For you did sympathize and suffer along with those who were imprisoned, and you bore cheerfully the plundering of your belongings and the confiscation of your property, in the knowledge and consciousness that you yourselves had a better and lasting possession (AMPC).

1 Peter 1:11: Searching what, or what manner of time the Spirit of Christ which was in them did signify, when it testified beforehand the sufferings of Christ, and the glory that should follow.

1 Peter 4:12-16, 19: Beloved, think it not strange concerning the fiery trial which is to try you, as though some strange thing happened unto you: But rejoice, inasmuch as you are partakers of Christ's sufferings; that, when His glory shall be revealed, you may be glad also with exceeding joy. If you be reproached for the name of Christ, happy are you; for the spirit of glory and of God rests upon you: on their part He is evil spoken of, but on your part He is glorified. But let none of you suffer as a murderer, or as a thief, or as an evildoer, or as a busybody in other men's matters. Yet if any man suffer as a Christian, let him not be ashamed; but let him glorify God on this behalf. ... Wherefore let them that suffer according to the will of God commit the keeping of their souls to Him in well doing, as unto a faithful Creator.

1 Peter 5:1: The elders which are among you I exhort, who am also an elder, and a witness of the sufferings of Christ, and also a partaker of the glory that shall be revealed:

Revelation 5:11-13: And I beheld, and I heard the voice of many angels round about the throne and the beasts and the elders: and the number of them was ten thousand times ten thousand, and thousands of thousands; Saying with a loud voice, **Worthy is the Lamb that was slain to receive power, and riches, and wisdom, and strength, and honour, and glory, and blessing.** And every creature which is in heaven, and on the earth, and under the earth, and such as are in the sea, and all that are in them, heard I saying, Blessing, and honour, and glory, and power, be unto Him that sits upon the throne, and unto the Lamb for ever and ever.

From *The Daily Light on the Daily Path*

June 30

Revelation 3:19: As many as I love, I rebuke and chasten.

My son, despise not you the chastening of the Lord, nor faint when you are rebuked of Him: for whom the Lord loves He chastens, and scourges every son whom He receives.—Even as a father the son in whom He delights.—He makes sore, and binds up: He wounds, and His hands make whole.—Humble yourselves therefore under the mighty hand of God, that He may exalt you in due time.—I have chosen you in the furnace of affliction. He does not afflict willingly nor grieve the children of men.—He has not dealt with us after our sins; nor rewarded us according to our iniquities. For as the heaven is high above the earth, so great is His mercy toward them that fear Him. As far as the east is from the west, so far has He removed our transgressions from us. Like as a father pities his children, so the Lord pities them that fear Him. For He knows our frame; He remembers that we are dust. (Hebrews 12:5-6, Proverbs 3:12, Job 5:18, 1 Peter 5:6, Isaiah 48:10, Lamentations 3:33, Psalm 103:10-14) [1]

---

1   Bagster, Samuel, *The Daily Light on the Daily Path* reading for June 30 from *Daily Light (Lite)* App © 2019 by Tap Tap Studio. (accessed 30 June, 2018).

Recommended Reading

Don't Waste Your Sorrows by Paul Billheimer

Prison to Praise by Merlin Carothers

Practice of the Presence of God by Brother Lawrence

The Final Quest by Rick Joyner

Foundations of the Supernatural Lifestyle by Pat Holloran

Switch on Your Brain by Dr. Caroline Leaf

Love Like You've Never Been Hurt by Jentzen Franklin

The Baptism of Love by Leif Hetland

Broken Children, Grown Up Pain by Dr. Paul Hegstrom

Life-Changing Books by Gwen R. Shaw

UNCONDITIONAL SURRENDER. Gwen Shaw's life story. Paperback ....#000102
.... • French #000102FR
DVD UNCONDITIONAL SURRENDER NTSC (North American format) .... #DGSN
DVD UNCONDITIONAL SURRENDER PAL (European format) ....#DGSP

Devotional Books

DAILY PREPARATIONS FOR PERFECTION ....Softcover #000202
    French .... Softcover #000202FR
DAY BY DAY— *A devotional based on the Psalms* .... • Softcover #000204
.... • Hardcover #000203
    French.. • Softcover #000204FR • Hardcover #000203FR
    German.. • Softcover #000204GE
FROM THE HEART OF JESUS — *A devotional based on the Words of Jesus.*
.... Hardcover #000207
GEMS OF WISDOM — *A daily devotional based on the book of Proverbs.*
.... Hardcover #000209
    French...• Hardcover #000209FR
IN THE BEGINNING — *A daily devotional based on the book of Genesis.*
.... Hardcover #000211
    French.. • Hardcover #000211FR

Classic Bible Studies

BEHOLD THE BRIDEGROOM COMETH! A Bible study on the soon return of Jesus Christ.
....#000304 • Italian #000304IT • Russian #000304RU
ENDUED WITH LIGHT TO REIGN FOREVER. Bible study on the eternal, supernatural, creative light of God... #000306 • French #000306FR
GOD'S END-TIME BATTLE-PLAN. Bible study on spiritual warfare ....#00035
    .... • Spanish #000305SP • French #000305FR • Russian #000305RU
IT'S TIME FOR REVIVAL. A Bible study on revival ....#000311 • French #000311FR
OUR MINISTERING ANGELS. A Bible study on angels .... #000308 • French #000308FR
.... • Russian #000308RU
POUR OUT YOUR HEART. A Bible study on intercessory prayer ....#000301
.... • Spanish #000301SP • French #000301FR
.... • Russian #000301RU • Italian #000301IT • Japanese #000301JA
REDEEMING THE LAND. A Bible study on spiritual warfare..............................#000309
.... • Spanish #000309SP • French #000309FR • Italian #000309IT
THE FINE LINE. This Bible study on the soul realm and the spirit realm..............#000307
....French #000307FR
THE POWER OF THE PRECIOUS BLOOD — A Bible study on the Blood of Jesus
....................#000303 • Spanish #000303SP • Chinese #000303CH • French #000303FR
....• Italian #000303IT • Polish #000303PO • Russian #000303RU

194

THE POWER OF PRAISE. Bible study on praise ....#000312

YE SHALL RECEIVE POWER FROM ON HIGH Bible study on the Baptism of the Holy Spirit. ....
....#000310 • Chinese #000310CH • Spanish #000310SP

YOUR APPOINTMENT WITH GOD. A Bible study on fasting ....#000302
.... • Spanish #000302SP • Chinese #000302CH • French #000302FR
.... • German #000302GE • Italian #000302IT • Japanese #000302JA • Russian #000302RU

In-Depth Bible Studies

FORGIVE AND RECEIVE. The epistle to Philemon ....#000406

GRACE ALONE. The epistle to the Galatians..#000402

MYSTERY REVEALED. The epistle to the Ephesians..#000403

OUR GLORIOUS HEAD. The epistle to the Colossians! ....#000404

THE CATCHING AWAY! The books of 1 and 2 Thessalonians...........................#000407

THE LOVE LETTER. The epistle to the Philippians..#000405

THE TRIBES OF ISRAEL. Bible Course ....• Binder #000501 • 13 CD set #CTGS1
.... • French #000501FR

Women of the Bible Series

EVE—MOTHER OF US ALL ....#000801

SARAH—PRINCESS OF ALL MANKIND ....#000802

REBEKAH—THE BRIDE..#000803

LEAH AND RACHEL—THE TWIN WIVES OF JACOB ....#000804

MIRIAM—THE PROPHETESS ....#000805

DEBORAH AND JAEL. God's "warrior women" ....#000806

Other Books by Gwen Shaw

ASHTORETH: Goddess of Lust ....#000615

GOING HOME... #000607 • French #000607FR

KEEPING GOD'S SECRETS...#000609

LOVE, THE LAW OF THE ANGELS .... #000601 • Spanish #000601SP

SIGI AND I ....#000614

SONG OF LOVE. The Song of Solomon .... #000401 • French #000401FR

SWORD OF LOVE..#000613

THE FALSE FAST ....#000602

THE HIGH WAY OF FORGIVENESS ....#000616

THE LIGHT WILL COME FROM RUSSIA..#000606

THE PARABLE OF THE GOLDEN RAIN.................... #000603 • French #000603FR

THEY SHALL MOUNT UP WITH WINGS AS EAGLES ... #000604 • French #000604FR

TO BE LIKE JESUS ....#000605

Pocket Sermon Booklets

BEHOLD, THIS DREAMER COMETH .... #000707 • Spanish #000707SP

BORN FOR SUCH A TIME AS THIS...#000720

BREAKTHROUGH ....#000708
DON'T STRIKE THE ROCK! ....#000704 • Russian #000704RU • French #000704FR
FROM PEAK TO PEAK ....#000718
GOD WILL DESTROY THE VEIL OF BLINDNESS......................................#000712
HASTENING OUR REDEMPTION ....#000705 • French #000705FR
IT CAN BE AVERTED .... #000706 • Spanish #000706SP
IT'S TIME FOR CHANGE...#000714
KAIROS TIME ....#000709 • Spanish #000709SP
KNOWING ONE ANOTHER IN THE SPIRIT.....................#000703 • French #000703FR
TEACH THEM TO WEEP .... #000716 • French #000716FR
THAT WE MAY BE ONE ....#000715
THE ANOINTING BREAKS THE YOKE .... #000710 • Spanish #000710SP
THE CHANGING OF THE GUARD ....#000719
THE CHURCH OF THE OPEN ARMS ....#000713
THE CRUCIFIED LIFE ....#000701
THE MASTER IS COME AND CALLETH FOR THEE.... #000702 • French #000702FR
THE MERCY SEAT .... #000711
THROW THE HEAD OF SHEBA OVER THE WALL....................................#000717

Books about Heaven

INTRA MUROS (Within the Gates) unabridged — *Rebecca Springer*.................#109101
PARADISE, THE HOLY CITY AND THE GLORY OF THE THRONE ....#104201

Children's Books

LITTLE ONES TO HIM BELONG ....#000901 • Chinese #000901CH
TELL ME THE STORIES OF JESUS ....#000902

Prophecies and Visions

THE DAY OF THE LORD IS NEAR: Vol. I - IV.................................. with binder #001000

Music

TREASURES IN SONG Sister Gwen's anointed music in beautiful arrangements. These songs tell her life story! Two pages of full color photos of Sister Gwen in ministry and travels...#000608

Prices are subject to change.
For a complete catalogue with current pricing, contact:

Engeltal Press
P.O. Box 447 • Jasper, ARK 72641 U.S.A.
Telephone (870) 446-2665 • Fax (870) 446-2259
E-mail books@eth-s.org • Website www.eth-s.org